Praise for *PlantPure Comf*

"This amazingly practical book makes it easy to enjoy the healthiest, tastiest meals you can imagine. You will find concise answers to all your questions, and plenty of tips on how to make cooking quick and easy. In Kim Campbell's hands, 'comfort foods' do more than satisfy your taste buds. These wonderful recipes give you the comfort of knowing you are doing the very best for your health and your family's health."

—Neal D. Barnard, MD, FACC, President,
Physicians Committee for Responsible Medicine

Kim is one of the finest plant-based chefs, who knows how to make whole food recipes taste exceptionally good. This isn't just a cookbook you will look at, this is a collection you will USE. So grab a tea and cozy up—this is comfort food at its finest!

—Dreena Burton, bestselling author of
Dreena's Kind Kitchen and *Plant-Powered Families*

"Perfect for any home cook, regardless of their diet! From arepas to zucchini poppers, *Plant-Pure Comfort Food* is bursting with mouthwatering, health-forward recipes that will leave your friends and family hungry for more."

—Dr. Michael Greger, author of *How Not to Die*
and founder of NutritionFacts.org

"The term 'healthy comfort food' feels like an oxymoron, like an impossible best of both worlds. Yet, Kim Campbell mastered it in this delicious, decadent, collection of mouthwatering, tempting treats. Not only that, but this book offers a wonderful guide to creating and cultivating an ideal kitchen and culinary techniques that are optimal for preparing nutritious meals anytime. With all of the plant-based cookbooks now ubiquitously available, this is a special one that should not be missed."

—Julieanna Hever, MS RD CPT, plant-based dietitian and author of *The Choose You Now Diet* and *The Complete Idiot's Guide to Plant-Based Nutrition*

"In addition to providing fabulous, easy comfort food recipes—she had me at pancakes—this entire book is comforting. The explanation of whole-food plant-based principles, the guidance on stocking the kitchen and basic prep skills for this way of cooking are so clear, it's as if Kim Campbell is with you in your kitchen—but the compliments you'll get from whipping up these dazzling dishes will be all yours."

—Victoria Moran, author of *Main Street Vegan*

"I've devoured most of the meals Kim shared in her first books and they are by far the most flavorful recipes in the plant-based space. But don't take my word for it, see the hundreds of reviews people have felt compelled to share on Amazon. They don't hold back on Amazon reviews either, you either got it or you don't. Kim has a gift and I am grateful she continues to share her culinary discoveries with all of us!"

—John Corry, producer of *Forks Over Knives* and *PlantPure Nation*

If you are looking to take your healthy oil-free cooking to the next level, you need this book! Kim Campbell is an amazing whole food plant-based recipe creator and she outdoes herself in this book. With recipes like oil-free cheesy nachos with jackfruit, cornbread topped Buffalo pie, and my new favorite healthy gluten-free fig cookies, these recipes are showing up on my table every week.

—Kathy Hester, author of *Gluten-Free Vegan Cooking in Your Instant Pot*, HealthySlowCooking.com, and PlantBasedInstantPot.com

"Kim Campbell has done it again! This is not just a great vegan cookbook, it is a great cookbook that just happens to be vegan. These delicious, easy to prepare recipes of classic comfort food can be enjoyed by everyone. Don't believe me, then just try the 'Cheesy' Jalapeno Poppers, Instant Pot Scalloped Potatoes, and Peanut Butter Cup Bars. The Muffin Formulator will change your life!

—*Chef AJ*, author, 45-year vegan, and host of the daily YouTube show *Chef AJ LIVE!*

"Kim is a treasure trove of valuable plant-based knowledge that she incorporates into delicious, nutritious recipes. These recipes are the backbone of the transformative work that she and her husband Nelson achieve in the plant-based community."

—Jill Dalton, host of the *Whole Food Plant Based Cooking Show* on YouTube

"According to the Oxford English Dictionary, comfort food is 'food that provides consolation or a feeling of well-being, typically any with a high sugar or other carbohydrate content and associated with childhood or home cooking.' In this cookbook, however, Kim Campbell harkens back to the original definition of comfort: 'providing strength and support' (like a 'fort' or 'fortress'). These delicious recipes will take you and your loved ones to a happy place while giving your body everything it needs to be healthy and strong."

—Howard Jacobson, host of the Plant Yourself podcast

"This is a wonderful addition to anyone wanting not only healthy whole food plant based recipes but delicious at the same time. These are doctor approved!"

—Dr. Laurie Marbas, MD, MBA, cofounder and CMO of Mora Medical

"*PlantPure Comfort Food* is perfect for anyone looking to adopt a whole food, plant based diet. The book is full of guides to help make your cooking journey easier, and recipes that speak to the melting pot that is American food."

—Chef Del Sroufe, Culinary Specialist at the T Colin Campbell Center For Nutrition Studies, author of *The China Study Quick and Easy Cookbook* and *The China Study Family Cookbook*

PlantPure

comfort food

Also by Kim Campbell

PlantPure Nation
The PlantPure Kitchen

PlantPure
comfort food

Over 100 Plant-Based and Mostly
Gluten-Free Recipes to Nourish Your
Body and Soothe Your Soul

Kim Campbell

BenBella Books, Inc.
Dallas, TX

BenBella Books, Inc.
10440 N. Central Expressway
Suite 800
Dallas, TX 75231
benbellabooks.com
Send feedback to feedback@benbellabooks.com

BenBella is a federally registered trademark.

Printed in the United States of America
10 9 8 7 6 5 4 3 2 1

Library of Congress Control Number: 2022013468
ISBN 9781637742273 (trade paperback)
ISBN 9781637742280 (electronic)

Editing by Leah Wilson and Karen Wise
Copyediting by Jennifer Greenstein
Proofreading by Sarah Vostok and Marissa Wold Uhrina
Indexing by WordCo
Text design and composition by Aaron Edmiston
Cover design by Sarah Avinger
Cover photo and interior food photography by Nicole
   Axworthy
Lifestyle photos by Brian Olson
Printed by Versa Press

**Special discounts for bulk sales are available.
Please contact bulkorders@benbellabooks.com.**

Contents

Foreword

We have known our daughter-in-law, Kim—the wife of our oldest son, Nelson—since she was in high school. We knew she had culinary talents when Nelson had to hide the delicious Boston cream pies she made in the back of the fridge to keep them away from his hungry brothers.

Now, four decades later, Kim has become a leading culinary developer and educator in plant-based cuisine. Her recipes are original, built from her knowledge and her intuition, often with an eye toward replicating familiar tastes and textures. We also know from firsthand experience that she is an excellent culinary educator. Her cooking classes have always been popular.

Today, the plant-based nutrition message is more important than ever. We have suffered through a pandemic that has not only caused an incredible number of hospitalizations and deaths but also imposed severe costs on our economies, communities, families, and—most vulnerable of all—our kids. It will take years for researchers to quantify all the damage. Unfortunately, there was an important message that went unsaid by our governmental, industry, and media authorities: that a whole food, plant-based diet can quickly reverse many of the chronic conditions that predispose people to the worst outcomes of COVID-19 or any other viral infection. This diet can also help strengthen our immune systems.

Whole plant foods are loaded with all manner of good nutrients, including countless phytochemicals that reduce our risk for chronic diseases such as heart disease and type 2 diabetes. And regarding the immune system, the well-known study in China directed by Colin—both the original in 1983 and the larger follow-up in 1989—produced fascinating data showing that people consuming more plant foods had in their blood less active virus from and more antibodies against hepatitis B, a dangerous virus that kills about eight hundred thousand people per year. More recently, three smaller studies specifically on COVID-19 showed similar results. This was not a surprising finding, because what is good for one part of the body tends to be good for all its other parts.

Communicating this empowering message to the public, though, is not enough to change people's eating habits. Kim and Nelson have learned this over the years in the work they have done with communities through PlantPure. People require access to delicious food to support their transition to a healthy diet. Unfortunately, too many people in the plant-based community have taken extreme positions, not well founded in science, that make it harder to develop and deliver good-tasting food to those who are used to a mainstream way of eating. Kim, on the other hand, has succeeded in producing healthy whole food, plant-based dishes with flavors and textures that traditional eaters love. Producing these foods has become Kim's lifelong mission.

We hope that you see in Kim's recipes what we do and that eating these foods will make the abstract idea of eating a whole food, plant-based diet real for you, in your everyday life. You'll come to understand that you can change your life and the lives of those around you by changing what you eat—and derive great joy in the process. Bon appétit!

Karen and T. Colin Campbell

Preface

I read my parents' foreword to this book and see they mentioned the Boston cream pies. Yes, it's true, Kim made these for me in high school and I brought them home and promptly placed them in the back of the fridge, out of sight of my brothers. They were delicious!

Over the years, I have watched Kim hone her culinary skills through countless hours of study and experimentation. Her family on her maternal side has a strong artistic streak, which has extended to Kim. Making great food is, indeed, artistry because it is intuitive. A recipe looks linear because you add A, B, and C to get D. But creating that formula is an artistic process. Often chefs just have a hunch about what would work well together, and they act on that hunch to create something that dances on the tongue, with just the right amount of texture and aroma.

I think it's safe to say that I am Kim's official taste tester, which is a fun job because her recipes are almost always spot-on. As I write this, for example, I suspect I may need to taste more recipes for her on Super Bowl Sunday. It's a dream job, even though it's unpaid!

Because I tasted every single one, I know the recipes in this cookbook are strong. I have told Kim that I think this third book may be her best. And what I love most about Kim's culinary work is that her meals not only have amazing tastes, textures, and aromas but are also life-giving. The phrase "food as medicine" is becoming more popular these days, but, of course, we don't usually think of medicine as joyful. Kim's food is healing and deeply satisfying at the same time.

Making a plant-based diet appealing is how we will build a plant-based world. For health, environmental, and other reasons, we need to make this change as quickly as possible. Whether we succeed or not depends on the food choices we offer people and whether those choices give them joy.

I am proud to be Kim's official taste tester and her biggest fan, and I hope you enjoy her beautiful recipes as much as I do!

Nelson Campbell

Introduction

Most of us have powerful memories of someone cooking for us. Cooking is a form of nurturing, and societies around the world have been "breaking bread" with their families, communities, and friends for centuries. The sharing of food creates a powerful human connection—a connection that becomes imprinted in our taste buds as much as our preference for particular foods or flavors.

Our food preferences begin forming in childhood and continue into adulthood, and explain why familiar smells, textures, and flavors dominate the choices we make today. The stronger our memories are of certain foods, the more likely we are to choose them. This includes our memories of food aromas, which often bring with them a flood of emotion.

These days, home cooking has become something of a lost art. Many of us have moved away from home cooking and instead allowed food companies to cook for our families. It's understandable. I am a chef, and even for me, it's nice sometimes to let someone else do the cooking. But when we do, we lose the opportunity to nurture our loved ones and we lose our connections to our family's traditional foods—whatever our family's cultural and culinary traditions may be.

I put much of this cookbook together during the early months of the pandemic. My husband, Nelson, and I previously enjoyed weekly trips to fun restaurants as a way to unwind and enjoy someone else's cooking. However, when home became a place we never left, we got creative. Instead of heading to a restaurant, we spent "date night" at home, making dinner together. I'm the main cook in our house, but the more we cooked together, the more Nelson's culinary talents surfaced. After thirty-four years of marriage, our shared time in the kitchen brought us closer together.

Though food nourishes the soul, the food many of us grew up with doesn't always nourish our bodies. The rates of preventable lifestyle diseases such as heart disease, type 2 diabetes, and obesity continue to increase, and we haven't been very good at making the connection between these diseases and the food we are eating. Our food choices continue to revolve around animal-based and processed foods. Meat and dairy consumption have tripled since the 1960s. Processed foods take up more than half of our grocery store shelf space and 75 percent of the average American's food budget. Fast, unhealthy food is the norm for many households, while more nourishing home-cooked food is an anomaly. And I am especially concerned about what we are feeding children in our schools. When I was teaching in the public school system, I witnessed firsthand what our children were being fed. Unhealthy food was the norm, which seems to run counter to schools' mandate to act in the long-term interests of their students. Rather than building early emotional connections to nourishing, healthful food that would serve them well for the rest of their lives, our kids are forming taste preferences for foods that research shows contribute to disease.

I love the opposite idea—feeding people nourishing food—and I love creating recipes that make good health flavorful. I'm also passionate about teaching culinary skills to others. My father, Carl Pearce, had a plaque on his office wall that read: "If you give a man a fish, you feed him for a day. Teach a man to fish, and you feed him for a lifetime." But, of course, I prefer something more plant-based: "If you give a person a meal, you feed them for a day. Teach a person to prepare their own plant-based meals, and you will nourish them for a lifetime."

Almost everyone in my family is an educator, so I guess I was always destined to teach in some capacity. I grew up in rural upstate New York and was raised in a home that was traditional in many ways, including in our food choices. My father grew up on a dairy farm and I was born on that same farm, so milk, cheese, butter, and eggs were staples in our fridge. My mother taught us how to cook, and we all sat down together for family meals. I grew up with traditional mainstream American dishes; almost every recipe contained meat, dairy, or eggs, so I grew to love their flavors and textures.

I met Nelson in high school, and I learned so much from his father, T. Colin Campbell, whose research focused on the health benefits of plant-based diets, that I started preparing plant-based meals shortly after we met. After that, I went to college to study dietetics and quickly discovered that Colin's research and ideas were not in the curriculum.

I'm the youngest child of four, and I think it's fair to say that my siblings thought of me as a rebel. So when I brought my new approach to food and nutrition back to my parents and siblings, my ideas were not well received. Still, as long as I was willing to cook for my parents, they were happy to eat whatever I prepared.

My relationship with my father, who passed away from cancer not long after I completed my previous cookbook, was difficult at times. I challenged him on many issues, and I must admit, I think I received some pleasure from this in my earlier years. Don't we all do that when we're young? He would get so frustrated with my dietary choices that we had words about it often. He fed our kids hamburgers when I wasn't looking, and I, in turn, put tofu and spinach in his lasagna and veggie balls in his spaghetti. This led to some uncomfortable moments, and the relationship I had with him was sometimes strained. Because I cared deeply about my father's health, I was frustrated and sometimes angry both with him for continuing to eat the way he did and with our government, media, and health care system, which always seemed to drown out my voice whenever I tried to convince my father of the powerful benefits of a plant-based diet.

When my father was diagnosed with prostate cancer in 1997, I tried to get him to consider a whole food, plant-based diet. He turned a deaf ear and continued ordering steak and ice cream. He survived the prostate cancer but was then diagnosed with colon cancer at the age of eighty. Unfortunately, the word *diet* was never mentioned by any of his physicians, who focused instead on conventional radiation treatments, surgery, and multiple rounds of poisonous and debilitating chemotherapy.

My father was no spring chicken, so all of those treatments were hard on him. When the doctors had no more "treatments" to offer and sent my father home to die, he finally asked for my help. I provided nutrition books, cookbooks, and kitchen tools and spent a lot of time with my mother, teaching her how to prepare whole food, plant-based meals. I even sent PlantPure frozen foods to them, which helped their transition. Sadly, the toxic effects of the chemotherapy and other interventions took their toll, and my father passed away on December 19, 2018. I loved him dearly and miss him very much.

I wanted to share this story because of the many discussions I've had with people who have had similar struggles. They ask how to handle family members who are not open to changing their diet. I didn't always handle this well because sometimes my emotions got the best of me, but I am not sorry I told my father the truth about nutrition. That's what you do when you love someone. Families can indeed be challenging, but it's essential to continue to educate, respect, and most of all, love them. To this day, I'm still working hard to encourage a few family members to embrace a plant-based lifestyle. Old habits and traditions are hard to break.

Many people have also asked Nelson and me about our kids and the challenges we faced raising them on a plant-based diet. They grew up in a town in rural North Carolina, where they were involved in everything from baseball, basketball, and soccer games to church suppers to birthday parties, sleepovers, and more—and food was front and center at almost every event.

We were always quiet about our food choices, but it quickly became apparent to everyone around us that we were eating only plants. We ate around the meat, scooped away the cheese, and tried our best to make it work. It wasn't always easy, but I found that what I had learned through my relationship with my parents helped me navigate these situations more easily.

It was most satisfying when I brought plant-based comfort food dishes to our community gatherings and those dishes were the first to go. Curiosity even led a few friends to our home for small personalized cooking classes. I started collecting their traditional recipes and converting them to healthier plant-based and oil-free dishes. (Several of these converted recipes are in this cookbook.)

Of course, when our kids were visiting other houses or eating at school, they did not always make the choices I hoped they would. Sometimes they traded away their lunches (I found out much later), had ice cream at parties, and politely ate what their friends' families served them at sleepovers. It was sometimes painful to watch, but I knew they had to make their own decisions.

It didn't take long for them to start noticing the consequences of unhealthy food choices, as they arrived home with stomachaches and unpleasant digestive issues, and fortunately they began making healthier choices independently. I remember our youngest daughter ordering a hot dog "without the dog, please," at a local baseball game and then putting ketchup, relish, and mustard into the bun with a pickle on the side. She was young but already becoming wise about her health.

While much of my motivation around food stems from my experiences with family, many of the recipes in this cookbook also came from my experiences with people in our PlantPure community.

Back in 2010, Nelson and I hired a chef and began conducting ten-day plant-based immersion programs for people across the country, in which participants were provided education and daily food support in order to demonstrate the whole food, plant-based diet's impact on blood cholesterol, blood sugars, weight loss, and energy. The biometric results of these early immersion programs were so compelling that in 2015 we released the hit documentary film *PlantPure Nation* in theaters in over one hundred communities across the country. (It's now available through streaming services and online, including on Amazon Prime, iTunes, and YouTube.)

We launched PlantPure and the nonprofit PlantPure Communities after the film's release, motivated by the goal of helping more people experience the benefits of a whole food, plant-based lifestyle. This has allowed me to engage in some culinary education, and many of my cooking videos are available on PlantPure's YouTube channel. I have also had the opportunity to develop even more recipes, but this time for food products sold in grocery stores. I like to tell people that I work in the test kitchen at PlantPure. As a child, I wanted to work for

Our eldest experiencing the joy of cooking.

a chocolate company, creating its recipes. Little did I know that I would someday have a much better job at PlantPure, developing hundreds of recipes, several cookbooks, and food products to help give people better health.

I wrote *PlantPure Comfort Food* to focus specifically on traditional comfort foods and included recipes spanning multiple cultural traditions. Our country represents a beautiful patchwork of different cultures, and helping others reconstruct and veganize their family's traditional recipes is one of my passions.

More than anything, I hope this cookbook is a helpful resource for you, enabling you to nourish yourself and the ones you love. We all have reasons for living plant-based, whether for our health, the environment, or the animals. Whatever our reasons, if we share them honestly and with love and model the lifestyle to our children, families, friends, and community members, we can plant seeds that will change lives.

I am thrilled and honored to share another cookbook full of plant-based recipes to delight your taste buds and warm your soul.

"It's a wonderful harmony. The plants make the antioxidant shields, and at the same time make them look incredibly appealing with beautiful, appetizing colors. Then we animals, in turn, are attracted to the plants and eat them and borrow their antioxidant shields for our own health. Whether you believe in God, evolution, or just coincidence, you must admit that this is a beautiful, almost spiritual, example of nature's wisdom."

—T. Colin Campbell

Pantry Makeover

A well-stocked and organized pantry fridge and freezer is every cook's best friend. Even if you're transitioning to a plant-based diet for the first time, a kitchen makeover doesn't have to happen overnight. Instead, I recommend adding slowly and stocking up as you go. Each week add to your pantry as you explore new recipes and soon you will be on your way. I recommend you start here:

Fresh Produce
- Seasonal fruits
- Seasonal vegetables
- Herbs

Grains
- Brown rice flour
- Brown, white, and wild rice
- Buckwheat
- Bulgur wheat
- Cornmeal/polenta
- Millet
- Quinoa
- Rolled oats
- White rice flour
- Whole-grain pasta
- Whole-wheat flour

Legumes
Dry
- Black beans
- Chickpeas (garbanzo beans)
- Kidney beans
- Lentils (red, green, brown, yellow, black)
- Pinto beans
- White beans (navy, great northern, cannellini)

Canned

- Black beans
- Brown lentils
- Chickpeas (garbanzo beans)
- Kidney beans
- Pinto beans
- White beans (navy, great northern, cannellini)

Nuts and Seeds

I recommend purchasing nuts and seeds raw or dry-roasted and unsalted. Nuts and seeds are often roasted in oils, so be sure to read the ingredient list to make sure you are getting oil-free nuts. Always store nuts and seeds in the fridge or freezer to prevent spoilage.

- Almonds
- Cashews
- Flax meal
- Hemp seeds
- Peanuts
- Pumpkin seeds
- Sesame seeds
- Sunflower seeds
- Walnuts

Nut Butters

- Almond
- Peanut
- Sunflower
- Tahini

Baking Ingredients

- Active dry yeast
- Baking powder
- Baking soda
- Cornstarch / arrowroot / tapioca starch

Sweeteners

- Applesauce
- Coconut sugar
- Date syrup
- Dried dates, figs, raisins
- Molasses
- Pomegranate syrup
- Pure maple syrup

Canned and Boxed Goods

- Coconut milk
- Shelf-stable unsweetened plant-based milks
- Tomatoes (diced, crushed, paste)
- Vegetable broth
- Whole-grain breakfast cereals
- Whole-grain crackers

Refrigerated Items

- Condiments: mustard, ketchup, chili sauce, lemon and lime juice, tamari or soy sauce, vegan Worcestershire sauce, miso paste
- Tofu, tempeh
- Butler Soy Curls

Frozen Foods

Frozen foods are a great option, and there are always new veggies becoming available in the freezer section of the supermarket. I recommend buying a variety of oil-free produce items, for example:

- Berries
- Broccoli
- Cauliflower
- Corn
- Edamame
- Greens
- Hash browns (oil-free)
- Onions
- Peas
- Sweet potatoes
- Vegetable blends (oil-free)

Vinegars

- Apple cider vinegar
- Balsamic vinegar
- Red wine vinegar
- Rice vinegar
- White vinegar
- White wine vinegar

Herbs and Spices

- Ancho chile powder
- Chile powder
- Chinese five-spice powder
- Chipotle chile powder
- Curry powder
- Dried basil
- Dried chives
- Dried dill
- Dried oregano
- Dried parsley

- Dried rosemary
- Dried sage
- Dried thyme
- Fennel seeds
- Garam masala
- Garlic powder
- Ground allspice
- Ground black pepper
- Ground cinnamon
- Ground cloves
- Ground coriander
- Ground cumin
- Ground ginger
- Ground mustard
- Ground nutmeg
- Ground turmeric
- Italian seasoning
- Nutritional yeast flakes
- Old Bay Seasoning
- Onion powder
- Paprika (smoked and regular)
- Red pepper flakes
- Sea salt

Equipping Your Kitchen

Having a well-equipped kitchen is the key to success and ease in cooking. Most people don't hesitate to spend money on computers, phones, vehicles, or washers and dryers, yet they consider kitchen equipment a luxury. Think of it as an investment in your health. The easier meal prep is, the less likely you are to dine out or purchase food from "corporate" food companies. And you'll end up saving more than you spend in the long run.

I have more gadgets than I ever want to admit, but I use them all. How you set up *your* kitchen for success depends on how much you want to invest and how often you plan on preparing meals. If you have a large family and your kitchen is always active, I would strongly recommend almost everything on this list. Chances are, if you are already a home cook, even if you have been making meals that are not necessarily plant-based, you already have most of the items listed. Make your kitchen work for you!

Knives and Cutting Boards: You don't need many knives: an 8- or 10-inch chef knife, a serrated knife, and a paring knife will cover most of your needs. If there is more than one chef in the kitchen, I would double up on the chef's knives because that's the knife you'll use the most.

High-Powered Blender: There are many brands of blenders out there, but the one I use most often is a Vitamix. It is a bit on the expensive side, but it will last for many years. And Vitamix offers refurbished blenders at reduced prices. If you can't make the Vitamix investment, I would suggest a NutriBullet (900 watts). NutriBullets are significantly less expensive but not as long-lasting and robust as Vitamixes. Even so, I went for many years without a high-powered blender, soaking nuts and seeds before blending, and was still able to create amazing sauces.

Food Processor: A food processor is my most-used appliance. I use it often for veggie burgers, piecrusts, dips, cookies, and veggies that I want to shred, such as cabbage, carrots, and potatoes. I bought my first Cuisinart food processor from the thrift store and loved it so much that I purchased a new one a few years later.

Pans: I have enamel-coated cast-iron pans and use them for everything. They retain and distribute heat well and they're perfect for sautéing vegetables without oil. The cooking surface is more durable than nonstick coatings and is perfect for high heats. They clean up easily and the smooth enamel surface keeps food from sticking. Le Creuset has beautiful pans in a variety of sizes, and they will last a lifetime. Other less expensive brands, such as Lodge, Staub, and Cuisinart, also offer enamel-coated pans. If you're looking for a lighter pan, I recommend a Scanpan. Scanpans are among the highest-quality nonstick cookware on the market today. Investing in quality pans will save you money in the long run.

Baking Stones / Pizza Stones: Baking stones last a long time and retain heat, so food heats evenly. They are heavy, which makes them hard to store, so I keep mine in the oven all the time.

Baking Pans and Dishes: There are various types, sizes, and shapes of casserole dishes to choose from, and I have them all, from metal to tempered glass (Pyrex) to ceramic and stone, and from 8 × 6 inches to 11 × 15 inches. It's a personal preference, but I believe the stone pans are the easiest to clean and last the longest.

Pressure Cooker: The Instant Pot is my choice for ease of use and versatility. These pots can do a lot, but I mainly use them for cooking rice and beans and making yogurt.

Springform Pans: I use springform pans for cakes and no-bake pies. You can buy them in various sizes, and they make removing cakes from the pan so easy.

Silicone Muffin Molds: These are great because the muffins come out easily even without oil. You can buy silicone muffin pans or silicone muffin cup liners, and both work great. If you don't want to invest, there are always paper muffin cups.

Parchment Paper / Silicone Baking Mats: These are important if you are baking without oil. Parchment paper is excellent for lining casserole dishes and bread pans to prevent sticking, and makes cleanup a cinch. A silicone baking mat is an ideal baking sheet liner for roasting veggies or baking cookies. They're easy to clean and dishwasher safe.

Nonstick Griddle: If you're a pancake or waffle hound, you're going to need one of these. I have a ceramic-coated griddle that has the perfect nonstick surface.

Air Fryer: An air fryer is a mini convection oven that I consider a splurge item. If you already have a convection oven, it's probably not necessary. I own a Breville air fryer and use it daily. Because it's small, it heats up quickly and requires less time to cook. It's a great way to get a crispy fried texture without all the oil. I make French fries in my air fryer four or five times a week. It's certainly a fun addition to any kitchen.

Microplane: This is the perfect tool for grating citrus peel, ginger, and garlic.

Box Grater: This basic tool is handy if you're grating small quantities; if you have a lot to grate, grab the food processor.

Potato Masher: I think this one speaks for itself!

Vidalia Chop Wizard: If I'm dicing a lot of vegetables for a recipe, I tend to grab this to reduce cutting time. It makes perfect cubes, and it is super easy to use.

Tupperware Chop 'N Prep: This little gadget saves a lot of time. It's a small bowl with a fitted blade inside. You add your items such as nuts, toast, or garlic cloves and pull the string. The string spins the blade, and very quickly you have chopped nuts, bread crumbs, or minced garlic. There are a lot of sizes to choose from online.

. . . And More: Whisks, spatulas, wooden spoons, kitchen shears, tongs, a lemon squeezer, a steamer basket, and mason jars all come in handy.

Dairy and Egg Substitutes

When adapting traditional family recipes, dairy is often the most challenging category of ingredient for people to replace. However, there are many recipe substitutions and products available that make this transition easier. And these simple swaps for dairy and eggs can create not only a healthier dish but also one that is tastier than the original.

Cheese: Cheese is loaded with saturated fats and casein, a milk protein linked to cancer and disease. When I need cheese sauce or spread, I use these substitutions:

- **Ricotta:** Tofu ricotta cheese tastes very similar to real ricotta and can be used in various recipes. You can find my recipe on page 60.
- **Parmesan:** Grind up walnuts or any nut you choose, then add bread crumbs and nutritional yeast in equal amounts.
- **Cheese Sauce:** My cookbooks have a variety of "cheese" sauces to choose from, and I recommend you keep one handy in the fridge at all times. You never know when you might need a cheese topper or filling.
- **Yogurt and Cream Cheese:** You can make your own plant-based yogurt and cream cheese with a couple of simple ingredients. Check out my soy yogurt recipe on page 36.
- **Store-Brand Vegan Cheeses:** Many of the vegan cheeses available at supermarkets today have added oils and are expensive. However, better products are coming out every day, so I hesitate to say that there aren't any healthy options out there. To date, the only brand I currently buy is Kite Hill.

Milk: This is probably the most uncomplicated substitution because there are so many plant-based alternatives. I recommend trying a variety of milks to find the one that best suits you and your family. Choose plant-based milks that have no added sugars and minimal added ingredients.

- Almond milk
- Rice milk
- Soy milk
- Hemp milk
- Oat milk
- Cashew milk
- Coconut milk

Buttermilk: Vegan buttermilk is perfect for baking because it produces a tender, light texture in baked goods while also adding a little tang and depth. You can use the following easy recipe to replace 1 cup of buttermilk:

2 tablespoons lemon juice or vinegar + 1 cup plant-based milk

I recommend using soy milk for the creamiest buttermilk, but you can use any plant-based milk you have on hand.

Egg Substitutes: Eggs are used in recipes to emulsify, bind, leaven, and give structure. I find the egg replacer you choose is a personal preference. I tend to use flax meal and chia seeds the most since they do not impart a strong flavor to any recipe. Here are a few suggestions for egg replacement:

- 1 tablespoon flax meal + 3 tablespoons water (allow to thicken)
- 1 tablespoon chia seeds + 3 tablespoons water (allow to thicken)
- ¼ cup silken tofu (best for brownies, quick breads, and cakes)
- ¼ cup pureed banana (this will give a definite banana flavor)
- ⅓ cup unsweetened applesauce
- ¼ cup unsweetened plant-based yogurt
- ¼ cup prune paste (puree prunes in a blender or food processor with a small amount of water)

Swap the Meat for Whole Plant Substitutes

A common tendency among people transitioning to a whole food, plant-based diet is to seek out recipes or meals that include a meat substitute. However, these products often contain isolated soy proteins, textured protein, oil, and excessive salt. I recommend these minimally processed fake meat alternatives:

- **Baked tofu or tempeh** are minimally processed and make great meat and dairy alternatives. Try marinating and roasting tofu or tempeh for the best results.
- **Mushrooms** (especially shitake) offer a chewy, meaty texture and are great at absorbing flavors. Slice them, chop them, or grill them whole. Mushrooms make wonderful gravies too.
- **Green jackfruit or young green jackfruit** can take on the appearance and texture of meat when cooked. Slow-cooking or roasting green jackfruit in your favorite sauce or seasoning yields the best results. Green jackfruit alone doesn't have a strong flavor, but, like mushrooms, it takes on the taste of what you add to it.
- **Butler Soy Curls** are 100 percent non-GMO soybeans grown without chemical pesticides. When rehydrated, they are very meaty and chewy. We like to use Soy Curls in barbecue sauce or chop them for a mock chicken salad sandwich. You can order Soy Curls directly from the company (ButlerFoods.com). Butler even provides some delicious recipes on its website.
- **Cauliflower and walnut rice,** seasoned with your favorite spice blend and roasted, makes for a great taco filling, pizza topping, or addition to casseroles and enchiladas. I like to use my food processor for speed, but it's easy to find frozen riced cauliflower in the freezer aisle or fresh riced cauliflower in the

produce department. Chop up the walnuts and then roast the cauliflower and walnuts on a baking sheet lined with parchment paper or a silicone mat.

- **Artichokes and beans** make sumptuous sandwich fillings. Chop or smash them well, and add your favorite oil-free mayo, celery, pickles, onions, and spices. For a "fishy" flavor, add some chopped nori sheets.
- **Wheat bulgur and lentils** are perfect ground beef substitutes for soups, stews, and chili.

Basic Ingredient Substitutions

airy, egg, and meat aren't the only ingredients you may need to substitute in the kitchen, and knowing how to replace some common items can prevent extra runs to the grocery store for missing ingredients. Remember that any replacement ingredient can alter the flavor or appearance of the original recipe.

Baking Powder (1 teaspoon)
¼ teaspoon baking soda + ½ teaspoon cream of tartar

Baking Soda (1 teaspoon)
1 tablespoon baking powder

Bread Crumbs (1 cup)
2–3 slices processed toasted whole-grain bread **or** *1½ cups processed whole-grain crackers*

Coconut Sugar (½ cup)
½ cup Sucanat **or** *½ cup light brown sugar* **or** *½ cup date sugar*

Cornstarch (1 tablespoon)
1 tablespoon arrowroot powder **or** *1 tablespoon potato starch* **or** *2 tablespoons tapioca flour* **or** *3 tablespoons rice flour*

Dates (1 cup chopped)
1 cup raisins

Fresh Garlic (1 clove)
⅛ teaspoon garlic powder

Fresh Ginger (2 teaspoons minced)
½ teaspoon ground ginger

Fresh Herbs (1 tablespoon)
½ teaspoon dried herbs

Ground Allspice (1 teaspoon)
½ teaspoon ground cinnamon + ½ teaspoon ground cloves

Ground Mustard (1 teaspoon)
1 tablespoon prepared mustard

Heavy Cream (1 cup)
½ cup cashews + 1 cup water (process until smooth)

Ketchup (1¼ cups)
1 (6-ounce) can tomato paste
3 tablespoons apple cider vinegar
1 tablespoon pure maple syrup (or other
    liquid sweetener)
¼ cup water
½ teaspoon garlic powder
½ teaspoon onion powder
½ teaspoon sea salt

Maple Syrup (1 tablespoon)
1 tablespoon coconut sugar

Miso Paste (1 tablespoon)
1 tablespoon tamari or soy sauce

Oil (½ cup)
¼ cup raw nuts
¾ cup water (blend until creamy)
or
¼ cup nut butter
¼ cup water
or
½ cup mashed avocado
¼ cup water

Tamari (1 tablespoon)
1 tablespoon soy sauce **or** 1 tablespoon
coconut aminos

Veggie Broth
Better Than Bouillon reduced-sodium
vegetable base + water **or** just water

Wine, Red
Grape juice or cranberry juice

Wine, White
White grape juice or apple juice

Worcestershire Sauce
½ cup apple cider vinegar
¼ cup molasses
2 tablespoons tamari or soy sauce
¼ teaspoon ground allspice
¼ teaspoon garlic powder
¼ teaspoon onion powder
⅛ teaspoon black pepper

No Oil, No Problem!

*C*ooking without oil can be a challenge at first, but it truly becomes second nature once you learn how. Your taste buds will also begin to adapt and adjust within just a few weeks, reducing your preference for oil. Why ditch oil?

- **It's empty calories.** There are no nutrients in a tablespoon or even a cup of extracted oils—there are only empty calories. There are 9 calories per gram of fat, compared to 4 calories per gram of carbohydrate or protein. That's more than double the calories without any nutrients, and these added calories contribute to weight gain, obesity, and a host of diseases.
- **It's a processed food.** Oil is a highly processed food. According to my father-in-law, nutrition scientist T. Colin Campbell, we should strive to eat whole foods, not artificial concoctions created by extracting a single element from a whole food.
- **It's the wrong kind of fat.** Our bodies need fat to survive, but it's easy to get plenty of the necessary fats by consuming a variety of whole plants. Nuts, seeds, olives, avocados, soybeans, spinach, tomatoes, broccoli, carrots, corn, and many other plants contain fat—and when you eat these plants in their whole form, you also receive all their other nutritional benefits. This is the right way to consume fat; eating processed oil is the wrong way.
- **You don't need it for great flavor.** There are so many strategies for building great flavor without using oil. As your taste buds and cooking skills begin to change, you will find this way of eating very satisfying.

Oil-Free Cooking Strategies

1. **Sauté using a nonstick pan to avoid sticking.** I like to use stainless steel pans or enamel-coated cast-iron pans. Get your pan hot, add your veggies, keep them moving by stirring, and use a minimal amount (1–2 tablespoons) of water, vegetable broth, juice, vinegar, or wine to deglaze the pan. (*Deglazing*

means removing and dissolving the browned food sticking to the pan.) Deglazing adds an extra layer of flavor to vegetables.

2. **Toss and roast instead of frying.** I like to season veggies in a plastic bag, shake to coat, and then roast. Potatoes, mixed veggies, tofu, tempeh, and chickpeas are easy to toss and roast.

3. **Use parchment paper or silicone bakeware/mats** when roasting or baking in the oven. This also makes cleanup easy.

4. **Skip frying and try breading.** Dip vegetables, such as sliced eggplant, zucchini, okra, mushrooms, or onion rings, first into whole-grain flour, then into plant-based milk, and finally into seasoned bread crumbs. Bake at a high temperature (400°F–450°F) until golden. Convection ovens and air fryers are also great for achieving crispy textures.

5. **For baked goods, make substitutions** for oil using vegetable and fruit purees (baby food purees work well), canned pumpkin, avocado, silken tofu, or nut butter.

6. **For sauces and dressings, replace oil with water or juice.** If a sauce or dressing doesn't feel as thick or viscous as you'd like, you can add chia seeds, avocado, nut butter, cashews or cashew cream, or tofu and blend until smooth and creamy. It all depends on the consistency you prefer.

Measurements and Conversions

US Dry Volume Equivalents

Less than ⅛ teaspoon (salt or dried herb)	Pinch
Less than ⅛ teaspoon (liquid)	Dash
1½ teaspoons	½ tablespoon
3 teaspoons	1 tablespoon
2 tablespoons	⅛ cup
4 tablespoons	¼ cup
5 tablespoons + 1 teaspoon	⅓ cup
12 tablespoons	¾ cup
16 tablespoons	1 cup

US Liquid Volume Equivalents

8 ounces	1 cup
1 pint	2 cups (16 ounces)
1 quart	4 cups (2 pints)
½ gallon	2 quarts
1 gallon	4 quarts (16 cups)

US to Metric Conversion

1 teaspoon	5 ml (milliliter)
1 tablespoon	15 ml (milliliter)
1 fluid ounce	30 ml (milliliter)
¼ cup	59 ml (milliliter)
⅓ cup	79 ml (milliliter)
1 cup	237 ml (milliliter)
2 cups (1 pint)	473 ml (milliliter)
4 cups (1 quart)	0.95 liter
4 quarts (1 gallon)	3.8 liters
1 ounce	28 grams
1 pound	454 grams

Temperature Conversions

F: Fahrenheit $\qquad$ $F = (C \times 1.8) + 32$

C: Celsius $\qquad$ $C = F - 32 \times 0.5556$

Fahrenheit	Celsius
250°F	120°C
275°F	135°C
300°F	150°C
325°F	163°C
350°F	177°C
375°F	190°C
400°F	204°C
425°F	220°C
450°F	232°C
475°F	246°C
500°F	260°C

Grain Cooking Charts

Stovetop

Grain	Amount	Liquid	Cook Time	Yield
Barley, Pearl	1 cup	3 cups	60 minutes	3½ cups
Bulgur	1 cup	2 cups	10–12 minutes	3 cups
Farro	1 cup	5 cups	30 minutes	3 cups
Millet	1 cup	3½ cups	25–30 minutes	3½ cups
Oats, Rolled	1 cup	1½ cups	8–10 minutes	1½ cups
Oats, Steel-Cut	1 cup	3 cups	60 minutes	3 cups
Polenta	1 cup	4 cups	20–25 minutes	2½ cups
Quinoa	1 cup	2 cups	15–20 minutes	3 cups
Rice, Brown	1 cup	1¾ cups	40 minutes	2¼ cups
Rice, Parboiled	1 cup	2 cups	20 minutes	3½ cups
Rice, White	1 cup	1½ cups	15 minutes	3 cups
Rice, Wild	1 cup	3 cups	60 minutes	4 cups
Wheat Berries	1 cup	3 cups	60–90 minutes	3 cups

Instant Pot

Grain	Amount	Liquid	Cook Time*	Yield
Barley, Pearl	1 cup	2½ cups	22 minutes	3½ cups
Bulgur	1 cup	2 cups	10 minutes (low pressure)	3 cups
Farro	1 cup	2 cups	7–10 minutes	3 cups
Millet	1 cup	1¾ cups	10–12 minutes	3½ cups
Oats, Rolled	1 cup	2 cups	3 minutes	1½ cups
Oats, Steel-Cut	1 cup	3 cups	3 minutes	3 cups
Quinoa	1 cup	1¼ cups	5 minutes	3 cups
Rice, Brown	1 cup	1¼ cups	23 minutes	2¼ cups
Rice, Parboiled	1 cup	1 cup	5 minutes	3 cups
Rice, White	1 cup	1 cup	5 minutes	3–4 cups
Rice, Wild	1 cup	2 cups	25 minutes	4 cups
Wheat Berries	1 cup	3 cups	30 minutes	3 cups

High pressure unless otherwise noted.

FAQ

Why don't you include nutritional facts in your recipes?

This is probably the most common question I've received after publishing my first two cookbooks. I cook whole food, plant-based recipes, which by definition are healthy foods. Nutrition facts cannot capture the holistic nutritional effects of these foods.

"Everything in food works together to create health or disease.
The more we think that a single chemical characterizes
a whole food, the more we stray into idiocy."

—T. Colin Campbell

Also, the numbers for a recipe can vary depending on the food brand you use or the software you use to evaluate the recipe. And calorie counting, which so many people like to do, is both unsustainable in daily life and not meaningful, because food calories are not all created equal.

Every plant contains unique nutrients. Eating a rainbow of plants, including a variety of them daily; avoiding processed foods; and cooking your foods from scratch are the best ways to optimize your nutrition.

How do you get enough protein?

As my esteemed father-in-law, T. Colin Campbell, explains, a diet rich in whole grains, legumes, fruits, vegetables, nuts, and seeds provides the optimum level of protein. There are many professional athletes who have discovered this and are now consuming a plant-based diet.

Do you use gluten in your recipes?

Many of my recipes are naturally gluten-free, but those that are not can usually be altered easily with gluten-free substitutions.

Why do I have to eliminate all oils?

Processed oils have no added nutrients and are empty calories that can lead to inflammation, obesity, and disease. Extracting individual food components from whole foods often creates unhealthy consequences. This is also true when we turn avocados to oil (1 tablespoon = 1–2 avocados) or olives to oil (1 tablespoon = about 40 black olives). On page 21 I provide tips for oil-free cooking.

Why do your recipes contain salt and sugar?

Adding extra salt and sugar to food is not necessary to our health, and in high quantities they can have a deleterious effect. However, as my father-in-law often argues, there is no research to suggest that a little added salt and sugar in the context of a whole food, plant-based diet has harmful health effects. We believe it is important that people are free to eat food with flavors they enjoy. We will not change the world around the idea of plant-based nutrition if we tell people they must give up the food they love for food that tastes bland.

Does preparing plant-based meals cost more?

That depends on what you decide to cook. In general, however, a plant-based diet is much less expensive. Affordable legumes, whole grains, and tubers should be the foundation of your diet, which you then supplement with fresh fruits and vegetables. You can also save money by purchasing foods, like dried legumes and grains, in bulk. Eating fresh fruits and vegetables that are local and in season is another easy way to save money, which you can leverage even more by buying more than you need and storing the extra in your freezer.

Do I need special kitchen equipment to cook this way?

Although I have suggested kitchen tools on page 11, I began cooking this way with just good knives, cutting boards, and an old-fashioned blender. It's always helpful to have the equipment recommended in this book, but it's entirely possible to cook delicious whole food, plant-based meals without it.

Breakfast

Breakfast Potato Casserole

Sometimes you need a leisurely breakfast casserole to impress your guests. This simple recipe uses oil-free frozen hash browns, which I always have on hand. For the vegetable filling, feel free to substitute any of your favorite veggies, such as broccoli, zucchini, peppers, and asparagus.

Prep Time: 15 minutes | Cook Time: 35 minutes | Yield: 6 servings

Ingredients

Veggies

8 ounces mushrooms (any type), sliced

1 (10-ounce) bag frozen chopped spinach

1 (20–26-ounce) bag frozen oil-free shredded or diced hash brown potatoes (such as Trader Joe's or Cascadian Farm)

"Cheese" Sauce

2 cups unsweetened plant-based milk

½ cup raw cashews

¼ cup nutritional yeast flakes

3 tablespoons cornstarch

1 tablespoon tahini

1 tablespoon miso paste

2 teaspoons apple cider vinegar

1 teaspoon Dijon mustard

1 teaspoon lemon juice

1 teaspoon onion powder

1 teaspoon garlic powder

½ teaspoon sea salt or to taste

¼ teaspoon black pepper

Topping

1 teaspoon smoked paprika

Directions

1. Preheat the oven to 375°F. Line a 9-inch square baking pan with parchment paper.

2. In a large skillet, cook the mushrooms and spinach over medium-high heat until the mushrooms are tender. Add water as needed to prevent sticking. Set aside.

3. Put the frozen hash browns in a large bowl.

4. Combine the cheese sauce ingredients in a high-powered blender and process until smooth.

5. Pour half of the cheese sauce into the bowl of frozen hash browns and mix until thoroughly combined.

6. Transfer half of the potato mixture to the lined pan. Cover the potato mixture with the mushrooms and spinach. Top with the remaining potato mixture, then pour the remaining cheese sauce over everything. Sprinkle the smoked paprika on top.

7. Bake for 30 minutes or until the top is golden.

Carrot Cake Pancakes

Spice up your weekend with these sweet griddle cakes infused with warm spices, which are perfect for a cozy, crisp fall morning. It's a great way to sneak healthy whole grains, carrots, and walnuts into a decadent breakfast treat. Grab your griddle!

Prep Time: 15 minutes | Cook Time: 10–15 minutes | Yield: 3–4 servings

Ingredients

1½ cups whole-wheat pastry flour

1 tablespoon baking powder

2 teaspoons pumpkin pie spice, store-bought or homemade (page 67)

1½ cups unsweetened plant-based milk

2 carrots, 1 roughly chopped and 1 finely shredded

⅓ cup unsweetened applesauce

2 tablespoons pure maple syrup (or other liquid sweetener)

2 teaspoons pure vanilla extract

½ cup walnuts, finely ground

Fruit sauce or fresh fruit, for serving

Unsweetened plant-based yogurt, store-bought (such as Kite Hill) or homemade (page 36), for serving

Directions

1. In a medium bowl, whisk together the flour, baking powder, and pumpkin pie spice.

2. In a blender, combine the milk, chopped carrot, applesauce, maple syrup, and vanilla. Blend until the carrot is fully processed and the milk turns orange.

3. Pour the blender mixture into the flour mixture, add the shredded carrot and walnuts, and stir until combined.

4. Heat a nonstick griddle over medium-high heat. Pour about ¼ cup of batter per pancake onto the hot griddle and cook until the pancakes are bubbly on top and the edges are slightly dry, 2–3 minutes. Flip the pancakes and cook until they are browned on the other side, another 2–3 minutes. Repeat with the remaining batter.

5. Serve with a fruit sauce or fresh fruit and yogurt.

Tips & Hints

If you prefer thinner pancakes, add 1–2 tablespoons more milk to the batter.

These pancakes can be made gluten-free if you switch the whole-wheat flour to oat flour and add 1 tablespoon cornstarch. The gluten-free version is slightly denser but still a delicious pancake.

Granola Your Way

Granola is made up of three components: dry ingredients, wet ingredients, and dried fruit. I like to customize this delicious oil-free granola to my personal preferences using a variety of pureed fruits and flavoring extracts.

Prep Time: 15 minutes | Cook Time: 1 hour | Yield: 9 cups

Ingredients

Dry Ingredients

5 cups rolled oats (not quick oats; gluten-free if necessary)

1½ cups any combination: nuts, seeds, quinoa, puffed grains, unsweetened coconut flakes, flax meal, and/or buckwheat groats

Wet Ingredients

⅓ cup pureed fruit: banana, unsweetened applesauce, canned pumpkin, or any other fruit puree

¼ cup unsweetened plant-based milk or water

¼ cup all-natural nut butter (such as peanut, almond, cashew, or sunflower)

¼ cup liquid sweetener (such as pure maple syrup, molasses, agave, or date syrup) *or* 6–8 pitted dates, soaked

2 teaspoons pure vanilla extract or other flavored extract

2 teaspoons ground spices (such as ground cinnamon, pumpkin pie spice, or gingerbread spice)

½ teaspoon sea salt

Dried Fruit

1 cup mixed dried fruit, chopped if large

Directions

1. Preheat the oven to 275°F. Line two rimmed baking sheets with parchment paper or a silicone mat.

2. In a large bowl, combine the dry ingredients.

3. Blend the wet ingredients in a blender until smooth and creamy. Pour the wet mixture into the bowl with the dry ingredients. Mix until well combined and thoroughly coated.

4. Spread the granola onto the lined baking sheets. Bake for 1 hour. Turn off the oven, but do not remove the granola. Allow it to continue to cool naturally and dry out for 4–6 hours, or overnight.

5. Mix in the dried fruit and store the granola in an airtight container at room temperature for up to 2 weeks.

Tips & Hints

If you add dried fruit to granola while it is baking, the fruit will burn. Always add dried fruit last to maintain its fruity sweetness and soft texture.

Simple Soy Yogurt GF

This delicious plant-based yogurt is an excellent addition to breakfast bowls, fruit, dressings, sauces, and dips. And you can even turn this healthy yogurt into a thick cream cheese–style spread! Making yogurt is a simple process that takes minimal effort. The flavor is tangy, and the texture is perfect every time. The only two ingredients I use are unsweetened soy milk and a vegan probiotic. I specify the brands of soy milk in this recipe because I have had the best outcome with these brands. If you can't find them, stick with soy milk that contains only soybeans and water, since added thickeners, fillers, and sweeteners will spoil the fermentation process.

Prep Time: 5 minutes | Culture Time: 48-72 hours | Refrigeration Time: 4–5 hours | Yield: 4–6 servings

Ingredients

- 1 (32-ounce) box WestSoy organic unsweetened plain soy milk or EdenSoy organic unsweetened plain soy milk, at room temperature
- 4 refrigerated vegan probiotic capsules *or* ½ cup unsweetened plant-based yogurt containing an active live culture

Directions

1. Pour the room-temperature soy milk into a blender and begin spinning the milk at a very low speed. Slowly add the powdered contents of the probiotic capsules (but not the capsule shells themselves) or the yogurt to the blender. Continue blending for 15–20 seconds to disperse evenly. Do *not* add any sweeteners or fruit to the yogurt at this point, or it will not culture properly.

2. Pour the milk into two pint-size mason jars (or one quart-size jar) and close with the lids. Wrap the jars in a towel and place them in a warm area (around 70°F–78°F) for 48–72 hours. If your home is cooler, the yogurt will take an additional 24–48 hours to fully culture. Yogurt is done when it begins to coagulate and thicken, and moves away from the edge of the jars in one mass when tilted. If you have a warm porch in the summer, you can place the wrapped jars in the shade, and it will

culture more quickly. I recommend placing the jars inside an insulated bag for best results.

3. Refrigerate the finished yogurt for 4–5 hours. It will continue to thicken as it chills. If you notice a bit of water (whey) separating on the top of the yogurt, you can either mix it in the yogurt when serving or pour it off. Store in the refrigerator for 10–12 days.

Tips & Hints

You can also make yogurt in an Instant Pot. Pour the milk into two pint-size mason jars and place the open jars on a rack in the pot. Lock the lid into place and close the pressure valve. Set the yogurt time for 10–12 hours. The longer it cultures in the Instant Pot, the tangier the results. I like to make yogurt before bedtime so it's ready in the morning.

For thick, creamy Greek-style yogurt, place a coffee filter or double layer of cheesecloth over a mesh strainer and spoon the yogurt into the filter. Place the strainer over a bowl to catch the liquid (whey). Cover and refrigerate for 4–6 hours. The longer you allow the yogurt to strain, the thicker the results. You can even create a cream cheese–like thickness if you strain for more than 8 hours. Season the yogurt with your favorite herbs and spices—we especially like ranch seasoning (page 67).

Lemon Poppy Seed Pancakes

We often start our weekend mornings with a special breakfast. I love lemon poppy seed muffins, so I had to create a pancake with the same flavors. The unique combination of Japanese sweet potatoes, oats, and quinoa is the secret to perfect pancakes every time. We love topping these amazing pancakes with a seasonal fruit compote.

Prep Time: 15 minutes | Cook Time: 10–15 minutes | Yield: 3–4 servings

Ingredients

½ cup uncooked quinoa, rinsed

1 cup rolled oats (not quick oats; gluten-free if necessary)

1 tablespoon baking powder

1¾ cups unsweetened plant-based milk

1 cup mashed cooked Japanese sweet potatoes

6 pitted dates, soaked

¼ cup lemon juice

1 teaspoon pure vanilla extract

Grated zest of 1 lemon

2 tablespoons poppy seeds

Chia seed fruit compote (see tip on page 40), for serving

Directions

1. Combine the quinoa and oats in a blender and process on high until the mixture resembles flour.

2. Add the baking powder, milk, Japanese sweet potatoes, dates, lemon juice, and vanilla and blend until smooth and creamy. You may need to stop the blender and scrape down the sides to incorporate all the ingredients.

3. Transfer the batter to a medium bowl and fold in the lemon zest and poppy seeds until evenly distributed.

4. Heat a nonstick griddle over medium-high heat. Pour about ¼ cup of batter per pancake onto the hot griddle and cook until the pancakes are bubbly on top and the edges are slightly dry, 2–3 minutes. Flip the pancakes and cook until they are browned on the other side, another 2–3 minutes. Repeat with the remaining batter.

5. Serve with the fruit compote.

Tips & Hints

If you prefer thinner pancakes, add 1–2 tablespoons more milk to the batter.

If you can't find Japanese sweet potatoes, you can substitute Hannah sweet potatoes.

Very Berry Chia Seed Jam

This recipe is so simple, and the secret ingredient is chia seeds. These little gems are packed full of nutrition and are the reason this jam will never fail. Choose your favorite berries—or combination of berries—and I promise you will never buy expensive jams in the grocery store again. Serve over toast, plant-based yogurt, oatmeal, pancakes, granola, or cereal.

Prep Time: 5 minutes | Cook Time: 10 minutes | Yield: 2½ cups

Ingredients

3 cups frozen blueberries, raspberries, and/or strawberries

2 tablespoons lemon juice

2 tablespoons pure maple syrup (or other liquid sweetener) *or* 5–6 chopped dates

½ teaspoon pure vanilla extract

¼ cup chia seeds

Directions

1. Put the berries in a medium saucepan and cook over medium heat for 5–8 minutes, stirring frequently. The fruit will begin to cook down into a sauce.

2. Break down the larger chunks of fruit with a potato masher or fork until you get the consistency you prefer. Stir in the lemon juice, maple syrup or dates, vanilla, and chia seeds. Remove from the heat and allow to cool.

3. Allow the jam to cool to room temperature and thicken. Store in an airtight container in the refrigerator for up to 3 weeks or in the freezer for up to 2 months.

Tips & Hints

You can use the same process to make a compote with the fruits of your choice. In a large saucepan, combine 1 pound fresh or frozen fruit, pitted and sliced as necessary, with ¼ cup orange juice. Bring to a boil over medium-high heat, stirring occasionally. Turn the heat down to medium and add 3 tablespoons chia seeds. Using a potato masher or fork, mash the fruit slightly until it reaches your desired consistency. Allow the fruit to cook down until bubbly, about 15 minutes. Turn off the heat and stir in 1 teaspoon pure vanilla extract. Cool and store as directed for the berry jam.

Get creative and add some spices and flavorings, such as almond extract, allspice, cinnamon, cloves, citrus zest, ginger, or nutmeg, to your jam or compote for an added burst of flavor.

If you prefer your jam or compote thicker, simply add more chia seeds, 1 teaspoon at a time.

Slow Cooker Apple Pumpkin Butter

Pumpkin butter is loaded with traditional warm autumn spices. These spices find their home in this thick, creamy, and smooth spread, which is wonderful on morning toast, muffins, oatmeal, and plant-based ice cream and parfaits. Note that there is no need to peel the apples since the peel contains lots of fiber and nutrients and will be pureed later in the process.

Prep Time: 15 minutes | Cook Time: 9–12 hours | Yield: 6½ cups

Ingredients

2 (15-ounce) cans pumpkin puree

1 pound apples (3–4 apples), cored and quartered

½ cup coconut sugar

2 tablespoons pumpkin pie spice, store-bought or homemade (page 67)

1 tablespoon apple cider vinegar

2 teaspoons pure vanilla extract

Directions

1. Combine the pumpkin, apples, coconut sugar, pumpkin pie spice, and vinegar in a slow cooker. Cover and cook on low for 8–10 hours.

2. Stir, cover, and continue cooking until the apples are tender, 1–2 hours. Stir in the vanilla and let the pumpkin mixture cool completely.

3. Transfer the mixture to a food processor or blender and blend until no chunks remain. (You can also use an immersion blender for this step.) Store in an airtight container in the refrigerator for up to 2 weeks or in the freezer for up to 4 months.

Tips & Hints

You can use any variety or combination of apples you like, but sweeter apples are especially nice for this recipe. I often put this recipe in the slow cooker in the evening before bed. By morning, it is almost finished. What a wonderful smell to wake up to!

Sweet Potato Waffles or Pancakes

Sweet potato waffles or pancakes combine warm fall spices with oats, quinoa, and sweet potatoes into a balanced and delicious breakfast. This recipe is also perfect for using up those leftover sweet potatoes!

Prep Time: 15 minutes | Cook Time: 25 minutes | Yield: 4 servings

Ingredients

½ cup uncooked quinoa, rinsed

1 cup rolled oats (not quick oats; gluten-free if necessary)

2 teaspoons baking powder

1½ tablespoons pumpkin pie spice, store-bought or homemade (page 67)

½ teaspoon baking soda

¼ teaspoon sea salt

1 cup mashed cooked sweet potatoes

1½ cups unsweetened plant-based milk

1–2 tablespoons pure maple syrup (or other liquid sweetener)

1 tablespoon balsamic vinegar

Fruit sauce or fresh fruit, for serving

Directions

1. Preheat a waffle iron until the ready light appears. (It's a good idea to continue heating the waffle iron after the ready light appears because a very hot waffle iron prevents sticking.)

2. Combine the quinoa and oats in a blender and process on high until the mixture resembles flour. Add the baking powder, pumpkin pie spice, baking soda, salt, sweet potatoes, milk, maple syrup, and vinegar and blend until well combined. You may need to stop the blender and scrape down the sides to incorporate all the ingredients.

3. Pour the batter onto the heated waffle iron and cook for 10–12 minutes. Do not attempt to open the waffle iron before 3 minutes, as this may cause the waffles to separate and stick. The trick is patience! When 10 minutes is up and there is no steam escaping from the waffle iron, slowly lift the lid. If any separation is occurring, quickly close the lid and give the waffles another 1–2 minutes. Waffles will not stick if you cook them until they are crispy on the outside, so adding extra cook time is an essential last step. Repeat with the remaining batter.

4. Serve with a fruit sauce or fresh fruit and/or additional maple syrup.

Southern-Style Polenta and Greens

We love polenta and grits in our family, and my husband requests them every weekend. (The main difference between polenta and grits? Polenta is made from yellow corn, and grits are made from white corn.) Nelson spent his childhood in the South and was raised by a southern mama, so he deserves a lot of the credit for this recipe. I took some lessons from him on seasoning up a pot of flavorful polenta and styled a cozy breakfast bowl packed with plenty of mushrooms and spinach for added nutrients.

Prep Time: 15 minutes | Cook Time: 20 minutes | Yield: 3–4 servings

Ingredients

Polenta

3½ cups water

1 cup instant polenta (such as Bob's Red Mill)

1 tablespoon nutritional yeast flakes

1 teaspoon garlic powder

1 teaspoon onion powder

½ teaspoon sea salt or to taste

¼ teaspoon black pepper

Veggies

1 medium onion, diced

8 ounces mushrooms (any type), sliced

4 garlic cloves, minced

1 tablespoon low-sodium tamari

1 tablespoon balsamic vinegar

1 (15-ounce) can white navy beans, drained and rinsed

5 ounces spinach, roughly chopped

Directions

1. In a medium pot, bring the water to a boil over high heat. Reduce the heat to medium-high and slowly stir in the polenta, nutritional yeast, garlic powder, onion powder, salt, and pepper, whisking continuously. If you add the polenta too quickly, lumps will form.

2. Reduce the heat to low and continue stirring the polenta for 1–2 minutes to avoid lumps. Cover and simmer for 15–20 minutes, stirring occasionally. If the polenta is too thick, add a bit more water and stir.

3. Meanwhile, in a medium skillet, sauté the onion and mushrooms over medium heat. (The mushrooms have a good amount of moisture, so you shouldn't need to add water to prevent sticking. However, if sticking and burning occur, add a small amount of water to deglaze the pan.)

4. Add the garlic, tamari, vinegar, beans, and spinach and cook for 1–2 minutes or until the spinach is thoroughly wilted.

5. Serve the polenta topped with the spinach and mushroom mixture.

Tips & Hints

You can replace the spinach with other greens, such as kale, broccoli, or collards.

Sometimes I like to top this dish with shredded carrots for added color and nutrients. Make this your own recipe and change up the veggies for what's in season or whatever you have on hand.

Chik'n Noodle Soup
for the Soul (page 54)

Whole Wheat Bread Bowls (page 89)

Soups and Stews

Black Bean Soup in Acorn Squash Bowls GF

This hearty, healthy meal in a bowl will surely warm you by the fire. I love the combination of sweet and spicy when the squash and soup come together. Baked acorn squash bowls go well with almost any soup style, so if you are in a rush and have leftover soups or stews in the fridge, bake a sweet acorn squash and make it a meal!

Prep Time: 20 minutes | Cook Time: 1 hour 15 minutes | Yield: 4–6 servings

Ingredients

4 acorn squash

2 tablespoons pure maple syrup (or other liquid sweetener)

½ teaspoon sea salt or to taste

¼ teaspoon black pepper

1 onion, diced

1 green bell pepper, seeded and diced

1 jalapeño pepper, seeded and diced

5 garlic cloves, chopped

2 (15-ounce) cans black beans, drained and rinsed

2 cups low-sodium salsa (such as Muir Glen)

1 cup low-sodium vegetable broth

1 tablespoon chili powder

1 teaspoon ground cumin

1 cup fresh or frozen corn

2 cups chopped fresh or frozen spinach

¼ cup chopped fresh cilantro

1 avocado, pitted, peeled, and diced

Directions

1. Preheat the oven to 375°F.

2. Cut the acorn squash in half lengthwise, or for smaller squash, cut off just the tops. Remove the seeds and pulp. Brush the inside and edges of the squash with the maple syrup and sprinkle with the salt and pepper. Place the squash halves cut side up on a rimmed baking sheet and bake for 30–45 minutes or until the squash flesh is tender when pierced with a fork. Remove and allow to cool slightly before adding the soup.

3. While the squash is baking, begin making the soup. In a large pot, sauté the onion, bell pepper, jalapeño, and garlic in a small amount of water over medium-high heat until tender, 6–8 minutes.

4. Reduce the heat to medium and add the black beans, salsa, broth, chili powder, cumin, and salt to taste. Cook for 10–15 minutes. While the soup is cooking, scoop out half of the soup and process in a blender until smooth and creamy. Return the

pureed mixture to the pot. (Alternatively, you can use an immersion blender to partially puree the soup right in the pot.)

5. Stir in the corn and spinach and continue cooking for another 5–10 minutes.

6. Ladle the soup into each squash half and garnish with the cilantro and avocado. Serve immediately.

Tips & Hints

You can fill baked acorn squash with almost any creamy soup or stew, such as the baked potato soup from The PlantPure Nation Cookbook*.*

Creamy Asparagus and Mushroom Soup

This creamy spring soup is hearty and flavorful enough for a one-dish meal. Just add your favorite bread, and you're good to go. The earthy mushrooms and spring asparagus tips combine to create the perfect textures for this delicious soup.

Prep Time: 15 minutes | Cook Time: 20 minutes | Yield: 4 servings

Ingredients

- 2 celery stalks, diced
- 1 onion, diced
- 2 small potatoes, small diced (about 1 cup)
- 1 (1–1½-pound) bunch asparagus, trimmed and cut into 1-inch pieces, tip pieces reserved
- 3 cups unsweetened plant-based milk
- 3 tablespoons nutritional yeast flakes
- 1 teaspoon garlic powder
- ½ teaspoon smoked paprika
- ½–1 teaspoon sea salt
- ½ teaspoon black pepper
- 8–10 ounces mushrooms (any type), sliced
- 1 cup low-sodium vegetable broth
- ¼ cup whole-wheat flour (or oat flour for gluten-free)

Directions

1. In a large pot, sauté the celery and onion in a small amount of water over medium-high heat until tender.

2. Reduce the heat to medium-low and add the potatoes, asparagus stems (do not include the tips), milk, nutritional yeast, garlic powder, smoked paprika, salt, and pepper. Cover and simmer until the potatoes are fork-tender, 10–15 minutes.

3. While the soup is simmering, in a small skillet, sauté the mushrooms over medium-high heat until tender. The mushrooms have a good amount of moisture, so you shouldn't need to add water to prevent sticking. Add the asparagus tips and sauté only until the tips become bright green. Set aside.

4. Combine the broth and flour in a blender and blend on high until smooth. Add the hot soup to the blender and continue blending until smooth and creamy. If you prefer your soup to have more texture, you can combine more or less of the vegetables until the desired consistency is achieved.

5. Pour the blended soup mixture back into the pot and heat over medium heat until bubbly and thickened.

6. Add the mushrooms and asparagus tips and serve immediately.

Tips & Hints

If asparagus isn't in season, you can substitute leeks or broccoli.

Taco Soup /GF

While I was teaching many years ago, there was a recipe floating around our school mailboxes called "taco soup." It began with ground beef as the base, and it called for an envelope each of ranch dressing mix and taco seasoning. I replaced the beef with Butler Soy Curls, and set out to re-create those seasoning packs by building plant-based ranch and taco spice blends. The resemblance to the original soup is pretty remarkable. The best part of this soup is its simplicity. My kids used to throw all the ingredients into a slow cooker in minutes.

Prep Time: 15 minutes | Cook Time: 50 minutes | Yield: 4–6 servings

Ingredients

4 ounces Butler Soy Curls

1 onion, diced

1 green bell pepper, seeded and diced

2 cups low-sodium vegetable broth or water

1 (15-ounce) can pinto beans, drained and rinsed

1 (15-ounce) can black beans, drained and rinsed

1 (28-ounce) can diced tomatoes

1 (4-ounce) can chopped green chiles

1 (4.6-ounce) can sliced black olives, drained

1½ cups frozen corn

1 tablespoon apple cider vinegar

¼ cup taco seasoning, store-bought or homemade (page 66)

3 tablespoons vegan ranch seasoning, store-bought or homemade (page 67)

1 teaspoon sea salt or to taste

Optional garnishes: unsweetened plant-based yogurt, diced avocado, sliced green onions, and/or crushed baked tortilla chips

Directions

1. Put the Soy Curls in a bowl and cover with warm water. Soak for 10 minutes or until fully rehydrated. Drain the Soy Curls and put them in a food processor. Pulse until they are crumbly. Set aside.

2. In a large pot, sauté the onion and bell pepper in a small amount of water over medium-high heat for 3–4 minutes or until tender.

3. Add the Soy Curls, broth or water, pinto and black beans, tomatoes and chiles with their juices, olives, corn, vinegar, taco seasoning, ranch seasoning, and salt and bring to a boil briefly, then reduce the heat to low. Allow the soup to simmer for 45 minutes. Serve with your favorite garnishes.

Tips & Hints

To make this soup in a slow cooker, rehydrate and crumble the Soy Curls as instructed. Put the Soy Curls and all the remaining ingredients in a slow cooker, cover, and cook on low for 4–6 hours.

Chik'n Noodle Soup for the Soul

Chicken noodle soup was the soothing and comforting "cure-all" food for every sickness during my childhood. This plant-based version is warm, cozy, and bursting with flavors that are sure to fix all of those aches and pains when you're feeling under the weather. But I love this soup even when I'm healthy! It's easy to prepare, hearty, flavorful, and loaded with veggies, noodles, and Soy Curls.

Prep Time: 15 minutes | Cook Time: 25 minutes | Yield: 4–6 servings

Ingredients

4 ounces Butler Soy Curls

1 large onion, diced

4 celery stalks, diced

3 large carrots, thinly sliced

3 garlic cloves, chopped

1 teaspoon fresh thyme or
    ½ teaspoon dried thyme

8 cups low-sodium vegetable
    broth

2 bay leaves

½ teaspoon sea salt or to taste

¼ teaspoon black pepper

8 ounces whole-grain noodles,
    fettuccine, or rotini (gluten-
    free if necessary)

¼ cup chopped fresh flat-leaf
    parsley

Directions

1. Put the Soy Curls in a bowl and cover with warm water. Soak for 10 minutes or until fully rehydrated. Drain and set aside.

2. In a large pot, sauté the onion, celery, and carrots in a small amount of water over medium-high heat until the onion is translucent. Add the garlic and thyme and cook for 2–3 minutes more.

3. Add the broth, bay leaves, salt, and pepper, stir, and bring to a boil over medium-high heat. Add the drained Soy Curls and pasta and cook for 10–15 minutes or until the pasta is cooked. Remove from the heat and discard the bay leaves. Top with the parsley and serve warm.

Brunswick Stew GF

We raised our kids in a rural southern community in North Carolina where church members cooked the iconic Brunswick stew and sold it to large crowds as a fundraising event. It's a tomato-based stew loaded with sweet and smoky barbecue flavors and chock-full of veggies. This vegan version of a southern tradition is thick, hearty, and satisfying.

Prep Time: 20 minutes | Cook Time: 50 minutes | Yield: 4 servings

Ingredients

1 onion, diced

2 celery stalks, diced

2 carrots, diced

1 large white potato, diced

1 (14-ounce) can young green jackfruit in water, drained and shredded

2½ cups low-sodium vegetable broth

1 (15-ounce) can diced tomatoes

¾ cup oil-free barbecue sauce (such as Bone Suckin' Sauce)

2 tablespoons vegan Worcestershire sauce

1 tablespoon Dijon or yellow mustard

1 teaspoon smoked paprika

1 teaspoon onion powder

1 teaspoon garlic powder

⅛ teaspoon red pepper flakes

¼ teaspoon sea salt to taste

1 cup frozen corn

1 cup frozen peas or lima beans

Directions

1. In a large pot, sauté the onion, celery, and carrots in a small amount of water over medium-high heat until the onion is translucent.

2. Add the potato, jackfruit, broth, tomatoes with their juices, barbecue sauce, Worcestershire sauce, mustard, smoked paprika, onion powder, garlic powder, red pepper flakes, and salt and bring to a boil. Turn the heat down to low and simmer for 30 minutes or until the potato is tender. Add the corn and peas and continue to cook for another 10 minutes. Serve warm.

Tips & Hints

Brunswick stew will have different flavor profiles depending on what part of North Carolina you are from. Some like it sweet and some like it a bit tangy, so keep in mind that the brand or flavor of barbecue sauce you choose will determine the outcome of the stew. There is no right or wrong way to make this stew, so select the flavor you love!

Pho Bowls GF

Vietnamese pho bowls are healthy, flavorful, and so simple to make. You don't need to head to a restaurant to experience a good pho bowl; in fact, most restaurant versions use loads of oils and meat-based broths. This pho bowl is loaded with fresh veggies, and when you start simmering the broth, your house will fill with the warming aromas of ginger, cinnamon, anise, and cloves. But it doesn't end with the veggies and broth; the garnishes are perfect for adding your own flavors and textures. I recommend offering the garnish ingredients in individual bowls on the table when serving, allowing people to garnish their pho however they like.

Prep Time: 30 minutes | Cook Time: 35 minutes | Yield: 4 servings

Ingredients

Pho

6 cups low-sodium vegetable broth

1 yellow onion, quartered

4 garlic cloves, peeled

1 (2-inch) piece ginger, sliced

1 cinnamon stick

6 whole cloves

3 whole star anise

½ teaspoon black peppercorns

1 tablespoon white miso paste

2 tablespoons low-sodium tamari or to taste

2 teaspoons rice vinegar

1 carrot, julienned or thinly sliced

½ head broccoli, cut into florets

1 bunch bok choy, sliced

12 ounces mixed mushrooms (any type), sliced

8 ounces wide rice noodles

Garnish

2 limes, sliced

¼ cup chopped fresh basil

¼ cup chopped fresh cilantro

¼ cup chopped fresh mint

2 cups mung bean sprouts

1 (14-ounce) package extra-firm tofu, drained and cut into 1-inch squares, or 2 cups frozen edamame

4–6 green onions, sliced

½ cup chopped peanuts

½ cup kimchi

Sriracha and/or hoisin sauce

Directions

1. In a large pot, bring the broth, onion, garlic, ginger, cinnamon, cloves, star anise, and peppercorns to a boil. Reduce the heat to low, cover, and simmer for 30 minutes to allow the flavors to meld fully.

2. Set a strainer over another large pot and pour the broth through the strainer. Discard the solids from the strainer.

3. Add the miso paste, tamari, vinegar, carrot, broccoli, bok choy, and mushrooms to the broth. Simmer over medium heat for 5 minutes.

4. While the veggies are simmering, prepare the noodles according to the package instructions. Drain.

5. Divide the noodles among four large soup bowls. Ladle the veggies and broth on top of the noodles and top with your choice of garnishes.

Tips & Hints

You can save time by purchasing ready-made pho broth in the international aisle of most supermarkets.

Lasagna Stew GF

Lasagna stew is everything you love about traditional lasagna but served in a comforting soup bowl. Hearty red lentils, warming flavors from tomatoes and Italian herbs, and a creamy vegan tofu ricotta cheese topping make this recipe an exciting twist on traditional lasagna. You may never return to layered lasagna again!

Prep Time: 30 minutes | Cook Time: 40 minutes | Yield: 4–6 servings

Ingredients

Stew

1 onion, diced

8 ounces mushrooms (any type), sliced

1 small zucchini, diced

4 garlic cloves, minced

¼ cup chopped dates

½ cup dry red lentils

2 tablespoons nutritional yeast flakes

2 teaspoons Italian seasoning

1 teaspoon fennel seeds, toasted

1 teaspoon smoked paprika

½ teaspoon sea salt or to taste

½ teaspoon black pepper

¼ teaspoon red pepper flakes

1 (15-ounce) can diced tomatoes

1 (24-ounce) jar low-sodium marinara sauce

5 cups low-sodium vegetable broth or water

8 ounces (7–8) whole-grain lasagna noodles (gluten-free if necessary), uncooked and broken into pieces

¼ cup chopped fresh basil

Vegan Ricotta Cheese

3 garlic cloves, peeled

1 (14-ounce) package extra-firm tofu, drained

¼ cup nutritional yeast flakes

1 tablespoon lemon juice

½ teaspoon onion powder

½ teaspoon sea salt or to taste

¼ teaspoon black pepper

¼ teaspoon ground nutmeg

Directions

1. In a large pot, cook the onion, mushrooms, and zucchini in a small amount of water over medium-high heat until tender.

2. Add the garlic, dates, lentils, nutritional yeast, Italian seasoning, fennel seeds, smoked paprika, salt, black pepper, red pepper flakes, tomatoes with their juices, marinara sauce, and broth or water and bring to a boil. Reduce the heat to medium and cook until the lentils are tender, 15–20 minutes.

3. Add the lasagna noodles and continue cooking until the noodles are tender, another 10–15 minutes. Turn off the heat and let cool slightly before serving.

4. Combine all the vegan ricotta cheese ingredients in a food processor and blend until creamy.

5. Ladle the stew into bowls and top with the vegan ricotta cheese and fresh basil.

Tips & Hints

Toast the fennel seeds by placing the seeds in a dry skillet over medium heat and stirring continuously for about 2–3 minutes, until golden and fragrant.

Irish Soda Bread (page 88)

Irish Colcannon Soup

Bring some Irish luck to your soup bowl! This recipe infuses sauerkraut into a bowl of traditional Irish potato and cabbage soup. This unique combination provides a bright, tangy note and is loaded with veggies in a delicate, creamy broth.

Prep Time: 20 minutes | Cook Time: 40 minutes | Yield: 4–6 servings

Ingredients

1 leek, thinly sliced

2 cups thinly sliced green cabbage (½ small cabbage)

2 carrots, small diced

4 cups low-sodium vegetable broth

1 pound red potatoes, cut into 1-inch cubes (about 3 cups)

1½ cups water

½ cup raw cashews

¼ cup whole-wheat flour (or oat flour for gluten-free) *or* 2 tablespoons cornstarch

2 tablespoons nutritional yeast flakes

1½ cups sauerkraut

½ teaspoon smoked paprika

½ teaspoon sea salt or to taste

½ teaspoon black pepper

2 green onions, sliced

Red pepper flakes, for garnish

Directions

1. In a large pot, sauté the leek, cabbage, and carrots in a small amount of water over medium-high heat until the leek and cabbage are tender, 10–12 minutes.

2. Add the broth and potatoes and bring to a boil. Reduce the heat to medium-low and simmer until the potatoes are tender, about 15 minutes.

3. Combine the water, cashews, flour, and nutritional yeast in a high-powered blender and blend until thick and creamy.

4. Add the creamy mixture, sauerkraut, smoked paprika, salt, and black pepper to the pot and stir to combine. Continue cooking over medium-low heat until the mixture thickens, 8–10 minutes.

5. Ladle the stew into bowls, garnish each serving with green onions and a pinch of red pepper flakes, and serve.

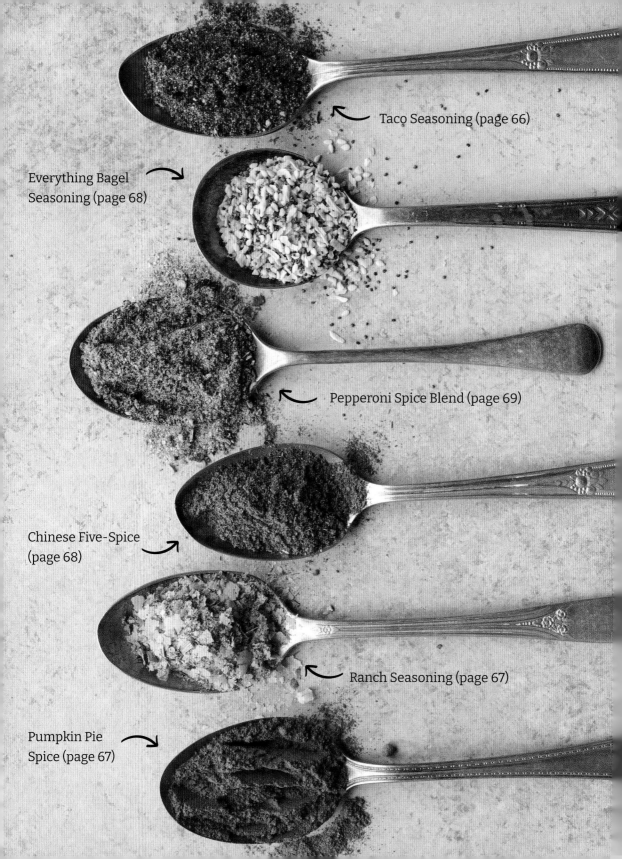

Taco Seasoning (page 66)

Everything Bagel
Seasoning (page 68)

Pepperoni Spice Blend (page 69)

Chinese Five-Spice
(page 68)

Ranch Seasoning (page 67)

Pumpkin Pie
Spice (page 67)

Spice Blends

Taco Seasoning GF

Homemade taco seasoning is simple to make, and you can easily customize it to your own taste preferences. It's a great way to save your money and health, as it's much cheaper than buying the packets that are often loaded with excess salts and fillers. This is our family's favorite combination of taco spices, with the perfect amount of spice and flavor. We love to add this seasoning to cauliflower taco filling, chili, beans, and plant-based cheese sauces.

Prep Time: 5 minutes | **Yield:** 5–6 tablespoons

Ingredients

3 tablespoons chili powder

1½ teaspoons smoked paprika

1½ teaspoons ground cumin

1 teaspoon ground coriander

1 teaspoon onion powder

1 teaspoon garlic powder

½ teaspoon dried oregano

½ teaspoon sea salt or to taste

½ teaspoon black pepper

¼ teaspoon cayenne pepper (optional)

Directions

In a small bowl or mason jar, mix all the ingredients. Store in an airtight container.

Ranch Seasoning

Most ranch seasoning packets are loaded with milk solids, excessive salts, and preservatives. This recipe is the perfect solution when you need a healthy version of a dried ranch dressing blend. This combination is a delicious addition to any plant-based mayonnaise or sour cream, creating a rich, creamy traditional dressing or dip.

Prep Time: 5 minutes | Yield: 7–8 tablespoons

Ingredients

¼ cup nutritional yeast flakes

1 tablespoon dried chives

2 teaspoons onion powder

1½ teaspoons smoked paprika

1 teaspoon dried dill

1 teaspoon garlic powder

½ teaspoon black pepper

¼ teaspoon sea salt or to taste

Directions

In a small bowl or mason jar, mix all the ingredients. Store in an airtight container.

Pumpkin Pie Spice

When it's pumpkin season, I like to put together my own version of this spice blend to flavor muffins, cookies, pies, granola, breads, and more. It's easy to adjust this recipe to your own personal preference. I love a little extra ginger!

Prep Time: 5 minutes | Yield: 5–6 tablespoons

Ingredients

3 tablespoons ground cinnamon

2 teaspoons ground ginger

2 teaspoons ground nutmeg

1½ teaspoons ground allspice

1½ teaspoons ground cloves

¼ teaspoon ground cardamom

Directions

In a small bowl or mason jar, mix all the ingredients. Store in an airtight container.

Everything Bagel Seasoning

This spice blend isn't just for bagels. It's an amazing blend of crunchy, nutty, garlicky, and slightly salty ingredients. We love to put it on flatbreads, hand-twisted pretzels, salads, roasted veggies, and more.

Prep Time: 5 minutes | **Yield:** 4–5 tablespoons

Ingredients

1 tablespoon black and/or white sesame seeds

1 tablespoon poppy seeds

1 tablespoon dried minced onion

1 tablespoon dried minced garlic

2 teaspoons sea salt

Directions

In a small bowl or mason jar, mix all the ingredients. Store in an airtight container.

Chinese Five-Spice

You can easily make your own Chinese five-spice blend if you don't want to buy a whole bottle. This is a unique spice that you might not find yourself using often, so creating your own blend is the perfect solution. It's easy to get hooked on this aromatic spice!

Prep Time: 5 minutes | **Yield:** 1–2 tablespoons

Ingredients

1 teaspoon ground cinnamon

1 teaspoon ground cloves

1 teaspoon ground fennel seeds

1 teaspoon ground star anise

½ teaspoon ground black pepper

Directions

In a small bowl or mason jar, mix all the ingredients. Store in an airtight container.

Pepperoni Spice Blend

This pepperoni spice blend is the perfect blend of spices for pizza toppings, sandwiches, and pasta dishes. We love to toss it with roasted cauliflower and walnuts, roasted tofu, or rehydrated Soy Curls. No more spicy pepperoni cravings!

Prep Time: 5 minutes | Yield: ¼ cup

Ingredients

2 teaspoons coconut sugar

2 teaspoons smoked paprika

2 teaspoons dried minced garlic

1½ teaspoons red pepper flakes

1 teaspoon ground mustard

1 teaspoon fennel seeds, lightly crushed

1 teaspoon sea salt

1 teaspoon onion powder

¾ teaspoon black pepper

Directions

Combine all the ingredients in a spice blender and blend until finely ground. Store in an airtight container.

Date Nut Bread (page 75)

Chocolate Zucchini Bread (page 78)

Breads

Arepas GF

Arepas are a staple in Latin America and are especially popular in Colombia and Venezuela. They are a gluten-free corn griddle cake made from masarepa, which is precooked cornmeal. They're crispy on the outside but tender and slightly doughy on the inside. You can top these fun little cakes with beans, guacamole, or even salsa. You can also slice them and stuff them with scrambled tofu, jackfruit, veggie taco fillings, or your favorite plant-based stuffing.

Prep Time: 12–15 minutes | **Cook Time: 20 minutes** | **Yield: 8–10 arepas**

Ingredients

2 cups warm water

½ teaspoon sea salt (optional)

2 cups masarepa flour

Directions

1. Preheat the oven to 375°F.

2. In a large bowl, combine the water and salt. Stir to dissolve the salt.

3. A little at a time, add the masarepa flour and stir with a whisk or your hands to make a dough. Your final dough should be moist and moldable (much like play dough) and will not stick to your hands; you might not need the whole 2 cups of flour. Once you have this consistency, allow the dough to rest for 8–10 minutes.

4. Using your hands, scoop out a fist-size portion of dough and roll it into a ball. Carefully press the ball between the palms of your hands to form a ½-inch-thick disk. Continue to form 8–10 disks.

5. Heat a large nonstick skillet over medium-high heat. Working in batches, add the arepas and cook for 2–3 minutes or until the bottoms are a deep golden brown. Flip and cook for 2–3 more minutes to brown the other side. Transfer to a rimmed baking sheet.

6. Bake the arepas for 15 minutes or until they are slightly browner. Allow them to cool slightly and serve warm.

Tips & Hints

Many mainstream grocery stores carry masarepa flour (Harina P.A.N. and Goya are the two most popular brands). It's important to note that masarepa is different from masa harina, which is used for making corn tortillas and won't work for making arepas.

Apple Pumpkin Bread

The delicious combination of apples and pumpkin makes this bread extra moist and perfect for autumn. It's ideal for breakfast, snacks, or dessert.

Prep Time: 15 minutes | Cook Time: 50–60 minutes | Yield: 1 loaf

Ingredients

2 cups white whole-wheat flour

1 teaspoon baking soda

½ teaspoon baking powder

½ teaspoon sea salt

1 tablespoon pumpkin pie spice, store-bought or homemade (page 67)

2 medium apples, peeled, cored, and finely chopped (about 2 cups)

½ cup walnuts

½ cup raisins

1¼ cups unsweetened plant-based milk

1 cup canned pumpkin puree

½ cup coconut sugar

2 teaspoons pure vanilla extract

Directions

1. Preheat the oven to 350°F. Line an 8 × 4-inch loaf pan with parchment paper, making sure there is enough overhang to easily lift the loaf from the pan after baking.

2. In a large bowl, whisk together the flour, baking soda, baking powder, salt, and pumpkin pie spice. Add the apples, walnuts, and raisins and mix until the ingredients are thoroughly combined.

3. In a medium bowl, whisk together the milk, pumpkin, coconut sugar, and vanilla.

4. Pour the wet ingredients into the dry ingredients and mix just until combined. Do not overmix. The batter should appear wet and lumpy at this point.

5. Pour the batter into the lined loaf pan and smooth the top. Bake for 50–60 minutes or until a toothpick inserted in the center comes out clean. Remove the bread by using the parchment paper to lift it from the pan. Allow it to cool for 15–20 minutes before slicing.

Tips & Hints

I recommend using a good baking apple such as McIntosh, Cortland, Rome, or Granny Smith.

This recipe also makes great muffins. Simply reduce the baking time to 20–25 minutes.

Date Nut Bread

Date nut bread is a traditional sweet, nutty bread that makes a perfect snack or a delicious breakfast muffin. This recipe was adapted from an old family recipe shared with me by Jeanne Schumacher, a PlantPure Pod leader and friend.

Prep Time: 15 minutes | Cook Time: 50–60 minutes | Yield: 1 loaf

Ingredients

2 cups pitted dates

1½ cups water

1 cup unsweetened plant-based milk

1 tablespoon balsamic vinegar

1 teaspoon pure vanilla extract

2 cups whole-wheat pastry flour

1½ teaspoons baking soda

¼ teaspoon sea salt

¾ cup chopped walnuts

¾ cup raisins

Directions

1. Preheat the oven to 350°F. Line an 8 × 4-inch loaf pan with parchment paper, making sure there is enough overhang to easily lift the loaf from the pan after baking.

2. In a small saucepan, simmer the dates and water over medium heat until the dates soften and begin to fall apart.

3. Transfer the date and water mixture to a blender. Add the milk, vinegar, and vanilla and blend until smooth and creamy.

4. In a large bowl, combine the flour, baking soda, salt, walnuts, and raisins and mix well. Add the mixture from the blender and mix just until combined; do not overmix.

5. Pour the batter into the lined loaf pan and smooth the top. Bake for 50–60 minutes or until a toothpick inserted in the center comes out clean. Remove the bread by using the parchment paper to lift it from the pan. Allow it to cool for 15–20 minutes before slicing.

Tips & Hints

This recipe also makes great muffins. Simply reduce the baking time to 15–20 minutes.

Banana Bread GF

I love a fresh loaf of moist banana bread that not only tastes amazing but smells delicious throughout my house. There always seem to be some overripe bananas in my fruit basket, and we love to put them to use in this recipe. Almond flour and oat flour give this moist bread the perfect texture, while the banana flavor speaks for itself.

Prep Time: 10 minutes | Cook Time: 45–50 minutes | Yield: 1 loaf

Ingredients

1½ cups oat flour

1 cup superfine almond flour (not almond meal)

¼ cup coconut sugar

2 teaspoons baking powder

1 teaspoon baking soda

1 teaspoon ground cinnamon

¼ teaspoon sea salt

3 ripe bananas

½ cup unsweetened plant-based milk

1 tablespoon flax meal

2 teaspoons apple cider vinegar

1 teaspoon pure vanilla extract

Directions

1. Preheat the oven to 350°F. Line an 8 × 4-inch loaf pan with parchment paper, making sure there is enough overhang to easily lift the loaf from the pan after baking.

2. In a medium bowl, whisk together the oat flour, almond flour, coconut sugar, baking powder, baking soda, cinnamon, and salt until thoroughly combined, making sure to get rid of any lumps.

3. In a large bowl, mash the bananas. Add the milk, flax meal, vinegar, and vanilla and mix well.

4. Slowly incorporate the dry ingredients into the banana mixture, stirring until the flour is fully incorporated. The batter will initially feel thicker than usual, but if you stir it well, the texture will be perfect. (There's no need to worry about overmixing here, since there is no gluten to cause the bread to toughen.)

5. Pour the batter into the lined loaf pan and smooth the top. Bake for 45–50 minutes or until the top is golden brown and a toothpick inserted in the center comes out clean. Allow the bread to cool in the pan for 10 minutes. Remove the bread by using the parchment paper to lift it from the pan. Cool for 10–15 more minutes before slicing.

Apple Pumpkin Bread (page 74)

Chocolate Zucchini Bread

Zucchini bread was always a staple in our house during the summer months when my father overplanted zucchini in his garden. There was no end to the creative ways we could use zucchini. I'm a chocolate lover at heart, so one of my favorite ways to use fresh zucchini is by turning it into a chocolate delight. Zucchini has so much moisture that there's no need to add eggs, oil, or butter to this naturally rich and dense quick bread. You'll love this moist chocolate treat for breakfast, lunch, dinner, or a snack.

Prep Time: 15 minutes | **Cook Time: 45–50 minutes** | **Yield: 1 loaf**

Ingredients

- 2 tablespoons flax meal
- 6 tablespoons water
- 1½ cups white whole-wheat flour
- ½ cup unsweetened cocoa powder
- 2 teaspoons ground cinnamon
- 1 teaspoon baking soda
- 1 teaspoon baking powder
- ½ teaspoon sea salt
- ¾ cup vegan chocolate chips, divided
- ½ cup unsweetened applesauce
- ½ cup unsweetened plant-based milk
- 1 tablespoon balsamic vinegar
- 1 teaspoon pure vanilla extract
- ½ cup coconut sugar
- 1½ cups shredded zucchini

Directions

1. Preheat the oven to 375°F. Line an 8 × 4-inch loaf pan with parchment paper, making sure there is enough overhang to easily lift the loaf from the pan after baking.

2. In a small bowl, whisk together the flax meal and water to make a flax "egg." Set aside to thicken.

3. In a large bowl, whisk together the flour, cocoa powder, cinnamon, baking soda, baking powder, salt, and ½ cup of the chocolate chips until well combined.

4. In a medium bowl, combine the applesauce, milk, vinegar, vanilla, coconut sugar, and zucchini and mix well.

5. Add the wet ingredients to the dry ingredients, along with the flax "egg." Stir until just combined; don't overmix.

6. Pour the batter into the lined loaf pan and sprinkle the remaining ¼ cup chocolate chips on top. Bake for 45–50 minutes or until a toothpick inserted in the center comes out clean. Remove the bread by using the parchment paper to lift it from the pan. Allow it to cool for 15–20 minutes before slicing.

Date Bread (page 75)

Muffin Formula 101

I rarely follow a specific recipe when making muffins, so when my youngest daughter wanted to make her own cookies and muffins, I created this simple template. Today she's the expert baker in our house, always surprising us with unique muffins from her own creative fruit, spice, and nut combinations.

Prep Time: 15 minutes | **Cook Time: 15–18 minutes** | **Yield: 10–12 muffins**

Ingredients

- 1 tablespoon flax meal
- 3 tablespoons water
- 2 cups whole-wheat pastry flour (or oat flour for gluten-free)
- 2 teaspoons baking powder
- 1–2 teaspoons ground spices (such as ground cinnamon, nutmeg, cloves, ginger, allspice, and/or pumpkin pie spice [store-bought or home-made, page 67])
- ¼ teaspoon sea salt
- 1 cup dried or fresh fruit (such as cranberries, raisins, dried cherries, fresh blueberries, and/or chopped fresh apple)
- ½ cup finely chopped nuts (optional)
- 1 cup unsweetened plant-based milk
- ¼ cup sweetener (such as pure maple syrup, coconut sugar, date sugar, or date syrup)
- 1 teaspoon pure vanilla extract or other flavoring
- ½ cup fruit puree or all-natural nut butter (such as mashed bananas, unsweetened applesauce, canned pumpkin puree, mashed cooked sweet potatoes, or almond/peanut/cashew butter)

Directions

1. Preheat the oven to 375°F. Line a muffin pan with paper or silicone liners.

2. In a small bowl, whisk together the flax meal and water to make a flax "egg." Set aside to thicken.

3. In a large bowl, whisk together the flour, baking powder, spices, salt, fruit, and nuts (if using).

4. In a blender or medium bowl, combine the milk, sweetener, vanilla or other flavoring, and fruit puree or nut butter and blend or whisk until smooth and creamy.

5. Add the wet ingredients to the dry ingredients, along with the flax "egg." Stir until just combined; don't overmix. The batter will have some lumps and dry spots, which is normal.

6. Fill the lined muffin cups about three-quarters of the way full. Bake for 15–18 minutes or until a toothpick inserted in the center comes out clean. Transfer the muffins to a wire rack to cool.

Tips & Hints

Muffin batter is typically thicker than pancake batter but looser than cookie dough. If your dough seems extra runny or too thick, simply add a bit more milk or flour to achieve the correct consistency. You can also adjust the sweetness by reducing the sweetener to your preference.

Strawberry Rhubarb
Streusel Muffins (page 82)

Sweet Potato Spice
Muffins (page 83)

Strawberry Rhubarb Streusel Muffins

When it's rhubarb season, I'm always looking for different ways to enjoy strawberries and rhubarb together. The rhubarb and strawberries give these muffins a very moist texture, and the cardamom and cinnamon make them extra special and delicious.

Prep Time: 15 minutes | Cook Time: 20–25 minutes | Yield: 10–12 muffins

Ingredients

Streusel Topping

½ cup rolled oats (not quick oats)

5 small pitted dates, soaked

¼ cup walnuts

½ teaspoon ground cinnamon

Batter

1 cup unsweetened plant-based milk

½ cup pure maple syrup (or other liquid sweetener)

½ cup unsweetened applesauce

1 teaspoon apple cider vinegar

1 teaspoon pure vanilla extract

2–2½ cups whole-wheat pastry flour

2 teaspoons baking powder

½ teaspoon baking soda

1 teaspoon ground cinnamon

½ teaspoon ground cardamom

¼ teaspoon sea salt

1 cup finely chopped fresh rhubarb

1 cup finely chopped fresh strawberries

Directions

1. Preheat the oven to 375°F. Line a muffin pan with paper or silicone liners.

2. In a food processor, combine all the streusel ingredients and pulse until you have a crumbly texture. Do not overprocess. Set aside.

3. In a medium bowl, whisk together the milk, maple syrup, applesauce, vinegar, and vanilla until completely mixed.

4. In a large bowl, combine the flour, baking powder, baking soda, cinnamon, cardamom, salt, rhubarb, and strawberries and mix well. Make sure the fruit is thoroughly coated and mixed into the flour mixture.

5. Add the wet ingredients to the dry ingredients, mixing gently until just combined. Do not overmix.

6. Fill the lined muffin cups with the batter and sprinkle some of the streusel on top of each. Bake for 20–25 minutes or until a toothpick inserted in the center comes out clean. Transfer the muffins to a wire rack to cool.

Sweet Potato Spice Muffins

These tasty muffins feature a unique blend of spicy and sweet flavors. Chinese five-spice powder is the perfect combination of ground cinnamon, cloves, star anise, and fennel seeds, making it a wonderful addition to quick breads and cakes. In addition, the sweet potatoes and almond butter give these muffins a moist texture.

Prep Time: 15 minutes | Cook Time: 20–30 minutes | Yield: 10–12 muffins

Ingredients

Streusel Topping (optional)

¼ cup rolled oats (not quick oats)

¼ cup walnuts

2 tablespoons coconut sugar

1 teaspoon ground cinnamon

Batter

2 cups white whole-wheat flour

1 teaspoon baking powder

½ teaspoon baking soda

1 tablespoon Chinese five-spice powder, store-bought or homemade (page 68)

½ teaspoon sea salt

1 cup golden raisins

1 cup mashed cooked sweet potatoes

¼ cup almond butter

1½ cups unsweetened plant-based milk

¼ cup pure maple syrup (or other liquid sweetener)

1 tablespoon apple cider vinegar

1 teaspoon pure vanilla extract

Directions

1. Preheat the oven to 375°F. Line a muffin pan with paper or silicone liners.

2. If making the streusel, in a food processor, combine all the streusel ingredients and pulse until you have a crumbly mixture. Do not overprocess. Set aside.

3. In a large bowl, combine the flour, baking powder, baking soda, five-spice powder, salt, and raisins and mix well.

4. Combine the sweet potatoes, almond butter, milk, maple syrup, vinegar, and vanilla in a blender and blend until smooth and creamy.

5. Add the blender mixture to the dry ingredients and mix just until combined; do not overmix.

6. Fill the lined muffin cups with the batter and sprinkle some of the streusel on top of each (if using). Bake for 20–30 minutes or until a toothpick inserted in the center comes out clean. Transfer the muffins to a wire rack to cool.

Sweet Potato Flatbread
(page 86)

Quinoa Flatbread

This recipe begins with just two simple ingredients: quinoa and water. The fun starts when you decide what flavors to add. The best part of this bread is how quickly and easily it comes together. I adapted this recipe from Jill Dalton, who has her own YouTube channel, *The Whole Food Plant-Based Cooking Show*. I didn't change the recipe's base but just added some extra seasonings that we like, and this recipe has quickly become a favorite staple in our house. We cut the flatbread into squares or wedges and top with our favorite dips, sauces, or veggies. It makes a great pizza crust too!

Prep Time: 10 minutes | Cook Time: 20–25 minutes | Yield: 4 servings

Ingredients

1 cup uncooked quinoa, rinsed

1¼ cups water

2 tablespoons nutritional yeast flakes

1 teaspoon onion powder

½ teaspoon garlic powder

½ teaspoon baking powder

½ teaspoon sea salt

2 tablespoons everything bagel seasoning, store-bought or homemade (page 68)

Tips & Hints

I like to add a handful of spinach, beets, or even a carrot or two to the blender for some extra color and nutrients.

Directions

1. Preheat the oven to 425°F. Line a rimmed baking sheet with parchment paper or a silicone mat.

2. Combine the quinoa, water, nutritional yeast, onion powder, garlic powder, baking powder, and salt in a blender and blend until smooth and creamy. The mixture should be the consistency of thick pancake batter.

3. Pour the quinoa mixture onto the lined baking sheet. Use a spatula to spread the batter evenly into an oblong measuring about 10 × 14 inches. You can also make four small flatbreads, each about 6 inches in diameter. If you like, sprinkle with the everything bagel seasoning.

4. Bake for 20–25 minutes or until crispy and golden around the edges. Allow the flatbread to cool slightly, then pull it away from the parchment paper.

Sweet Potato Flatbread

I love Indian flatbreads, and there is certainly a variety to choose from. Most Indian restaurants serve roti, but they use a lot of butter and oil, which can easily be omitted. The added sweet potatoes and spices make this roti a bread you will love for just about any meal. Serve with your favorite soups and stews, or use them as sandwich wraps.

Prep Time: 30 minutes | **Cook Time: 5–8 minutes** | **Yield: 4 servings**

Ingredients

1½ cups mashed cooked sweet potatoes (about 2 sweet potatoes)

1¾ cups whole-wheat flour, plus more as needed

1 teaspoon baking powder

1 teaspoon chili powder

½ teaspoon garlic powder

¼–½ teaspoon sea salt

¼ teaspoon ground cinnamon

⅛ teaspoon ground cardamom

Directions

1. Put the mashed sweet potatoes in a medium bowl.

2. In a small bowl, whisk together the flour, baking powder, chili powder, garlic powder, salt, cinnamon, and cardamom.

3. Add half of the flour mixture to the sweet potatoes and mix until the flour is well incorporated. Add the remaining flour mixture and combine with your hands until a dough begins to form. If the mixture is too wet and sticky, add 3–4 tablespoons more flour.

4. Cover the dough with a towel and allow to rest for 15 minutes.

5. Divide the dough into 6 equal pieces. Place a sheet of parchment paper on a work surface and dust it with flour. Roll each dough piece into a circle 5–6 inches in diameter, flipping the flatbread occasionally and dusting it and the rolling pin with flour if it begins to stick.

6. Preheat a nonstick griddle over medium-high heat. Working in batches, place the flatbreads on

the griddle and cook for 1–2 minutes. You will notice bubbles forming as they begin to cook inside. Flip and cook for another 1–2 minutes. As the flatbreads are finished, stack them and cover them with a towel to keep them soft and warm.

7. Store leftovers in a zip-top plastic bag.

Tips & Hints

You can also use oat flour in this recipe, but the dough will be much more delicate to work with and may be slightly more difficult to roll. Oat flour also creates a more delicate final wrap, but the taste is still amazing.

Irish Soda Bread

Irish soda bread is the perfect no-yeast bread—it is made with simple ingredients that produce a rustic, hearty, and perfect loaf. You'll want to eat this right out of the oven!

Prep Time: 15 minutes | Cook Time: 30 minutes | Yield: 6–8 servings

Ingredients

1¾ cups unsweetened plant-based milk (preferably soy)

2 tablespoons lemon juice

3 cups white whole-wheat flour

2 tablespoons coconut sugar

2 teaspoons baking soda

½ teaspoon sea salt

½ cup raw nuts and/or seeds

½ cup golden raisins

Directions

1. Preheat the oven to 425°F. Line a rimmed baking sheet with parchment paper or a silicone mat.

2. In a medium bowl, whisk together the milk and lemon juice. Set aside for 5–10 minutes or until the mixture becomes thick, like buttermilk.

3. In a large bowl, whisk together the flour, coconut sugar, baking soda, salt, nuts and/or seeds, and raisins. Form a well in the center of the flour mixture and pour in the "buttermilk" mixture.

4. Stir the dough with a spatula and use your hands to gently bring the dough together until the flour is just moistened. Form a rough, shaggy ball, but don't overwork the dough. If the dough feels too sticky, add a bit more flour as needed. It's important not to overknead, because this will activate the gluten and result in tough bread.

5. Transfer the dough to the lined baking sheet and flatten it slightly with your hands. Using a serrated knife, cut an X on the top about 1 inch deep. This will allow the center of the bread to cook.

6. Bake for 30–35 minutes or until a sharp knife inserted in the center comes out clean. When you tap the loaf, it should sound hollow. Cool for 5–10 minutes and serve warm.

Whole-Wheat Bread Bowls

Hearty soup or stew served in a bread bowl is a fun way to enjoy a warming meal. We often serve bread bowl soup for guests and pair it with a salad because it feels fancy and it's pretty darn filling too. This recipe can also be used for pizza crust, so if a bowl isn't your thing, grab some pizza sauce and a few veggie toppers and enjoy.

Prep Time: 1 hour 45 minutes (includes rising time) | Cook Time: 30 minutes | Yield: 4–6 bread bowls

Ingredients

- 1 tablespoon active dry yeast
- 2 cups warm water
- 2 tablespoons plus 1 teaspoon pure maple syrup (or other liquid sweetener), divided
- 3½–4 cups white whole-wheat flour
- 2 tablespoons vital wheat gluten
- 1 teaspoon sea salt
- 2 tablespoons unsweetened plant-based milk

Directions

1. In a large bowl, combine the yeast, water, and 2 tablespoons of the maple syrup. Let stand until frothy.

2. Stir in the flour, wheat gluten, and salt to make a soft dough. Knead until smooth and elastic, 6–8 minutes.

3. Place the dough in a clean bowl and cover with a damp towel. Set aside in a warm place to rise until the dough doubles in size, about 1 hour.

4. Line a rimmed baking sheet with parchment paper or a silicone mat. Punch down the dough and divide it into 4–6 equal parts. Form and stretch each part into a smooth, tight ball. Place on the lined baking sheet and use a sharp knife to cut an X on the top of each ball. Cover with damp paper towels and let rise until doubled in size, about 20 minutes.

5. Preheat the oven to 425°F.

6. Whisk together the milk and remaining 1 teaspoon maple syrup. Lightly brush each dough ball with the mixture. Bake for 25–30 minutes or until golden brown.

7. Let the loaves cool until they are easy to handle. Cut a ½-inch-thick slice from the top of each loaf. Scoop out the center (save the center to dunk into the soup) until you have a bowl big enough to hold your soup. Fill with your favorite soup and enjoy!

Hand-Twisted Soft Pretzels

Soft pretzels are fun to create—and irresistible to eat. The baking soda bath and toppings give these pretzels their traditional flavor, making them a hit in our house. They're soft and chewy on the inside and golden brown on the outside. Kids and adults love to roll the dough and form their own pretzels or unique shapes. Top them with anything you love for a great snack or appetizer.

Prep Time: 1 hour 15 minutes (includes rising time) |
Cook Time: 15 minutes | Yield: 10 pretzels

Ingredients

Dough

1¾ cups lukewarm water

¼ cup coconut sugar

1 tablespoon active dry yeast

2 cups all-purpose flour

2 cups white whole-wheat flour or regular whole-wheat flour

1½ teaspoons sea salt

¼ cup everything bagel seasoning, store-bought or homemade (page 68)

Mustard, marinara sauce, or Vegan Nacho Sauce (page 116), for serving

Baking Soda Bath

7 cups water

¼ cup baking soda

Directions

1. In a large bowl, combine the lukewarm water, coconut sugar, and yeast. Let stand until frothy.

2. Add both flours and the salt and stir until a soft dough begins to form. Knead for 6–8 minutes, until smooth. Place the dough in a clean bowl and cover with a damp towel. Set aside in a warm place until the dough doubles in size, about 1 hour.

3. Preheat the oven to 425°F. Line two rimmed baking sheets with parchment paper or silicone mats.

4. To make the baking soda bath, in a large saucepan, bring the water to a rolling boil over medium-high heat. Add the baking soda and allow it to foam.

5. Punch down the dough and remove it from the bowl. Cut into 10 even pieces. Roll each dough piece into a 22–24-inch rope. Bend the rope into a U shape, then twist and bring the ends down to create the classic pretzel shape. Press lightly to seal the ends. (Or get creative and make your own shapes.)

6. Drop one pretzel at a time into the baking soda bath and boil for 30 seconds. Remove the pretzel using a slotted spoon and transfer to the lined baking sheet. Sprinkle with the everything bagel seasoning.

7. Bake for 10–12 minutes or until golden brown. Serve warm, with your favorite dipping sauce.

Sandwiches and Wraps

Pulled BBQ Mushroom Sandwiches

When I saw all the recipes swirling around the internet using king oyster mushrooms, I wanted to see what all the hype was about. With a meaty texture and fantastic ability to absorb flavor, plus thick stems that shred into perfect "pulled pork" pieces, these mushrooms are truly special. The culinary possibilities seem endless (my foodie brain imagines tacos, crab cakes, scallops, and Philly cheesesteak sandwiches . . .), but I decided to stick with the traditional BBQ sandwich. The only challenge may be finding king oyster mushrooms in your local grocery stores. I found them at our local Asian market.

Prep Time: 20 minutes | Cook Time: 20 minutes | Yield: 4–5 servings

Ingredients

- 1½ pounds king oyster mushrooms
- ½ teaspoon smoked paprika
- ½ teaspoon onion powder
- ½ teaspoon garlic powder
- ¾ cup oil-free barbecue sauce (such as Bone Suckin' Sauce), plus more for serving
- 4–5 whole-wheat buns (gluten-free if necessary)
- 2 cups coleslaw

Directions

1. Preheat the oven to 400°F. Line a rimmed baking sheet with parchment paper or a silicone mat.

2. Slice the mushrooms in half lengthwise. Using a fork, shred the mushrooms by raking down the mushroom stalk to the base of the mushroom. Continue doing this until the entire mushroom stem is shredded. The tops don't shred like the stems, so remove the tops and slice them thinly. You will use the whole mushroom for this recipe.

3. Put the shredded mushrooms and sliced tops in a large bowl. Add the smoked paprika, onion powder, and garlic powder and toss until the mushrooms are well coated. Transfer the mushrooms to the lined baking sheet and bake for 15–20 minutes or until crispy and slightly golden around the edges.

4. Put the mushrooms in a large bowl and toss with the barbecue sauce.

5. Serve the BBQ mushrooms on the buns, topped with coleslaw and extra barbecue sauce.

Soy Curl Chik'n Salad

Many of us remember the classic chicken salad that was a favorite sandwich filling. I've got the perfect replacement recipe: a knock-your-socks-off salad featuring Soy Curls, vegan mayonnaise, veggies, and herbs. Soy Curls have a meaty, chewy texture that will fool your most avid meat-eating friends. Serve on bread or rolls with your favorite toppings—we like lettuce, sprouts, sliced tomato, cucumber, and red onion.

Prep time: 20 minutes | Yield: 4 servings

Ingredients

4 ounces Butler Soy Curls

¾–1 cup vegan mayonnaise, store-bought or homemade (page 131)

2 teaspoons lemon juice

2 celery stalks, small diced

1 carrot, shredded

3 green onions, sliced

¼ cup chopped dill pickles or dill pickle relish

1 cup seedless red or green grapes, chopped

2 tablespoons chopped fresh dill

2 teaspoons Dijon mustard

½ teaspoon sea salt or to taste

¼ teaspoon black pepper

Directions

1. Put the Soy Curls in a bowl and cover with warm water. Soak for 10 minutes or until fully rehydrated. Drain and squeeze out the excess water. Pulse the Soy Curls in a food processor until a fine texture is achieved.

2. In a medium bowl, combine the Soy Curls, mayonnaise, lemon juice, celery, carrot, green onions, pickles, grapes, dill, mustard, salt, and pepper. Mix until the ingredients are well combined. Serve immediately as a sandwich, wrap, or salad. Store in an airtight container in the refrigerator for up to 5 days.

Tips & Hints

I recommend you store Soy Curls in the refrigerator or freezer to keep them fresh. Soy Curls are an all-natural product that does not contain any preservatives or additives. They also have natural fats and will go rancid if stored in your pantry for long periods.

You can substitute smashed chickpeas for the Soy Curls.

Walnut Pesto Burgers GF

Pesto makes everything taste great, including veggie burgers. The olives, walnuts, and lentils create the perfect texture for this flavor-packed burger. We like to top our burgers with sliced avocado, pickles, onions, tomato, sprouts, or lettuce. I sometimes use this recipe to make veggie balls for a unique addition to spaghetti and marinara sauce.

Prep Time: 15 minutes | **Cook Time: 20 minutes** | **Yield: 6 burgers**

Ingredients

½ cup walnuts

1 (6-ounce) can pitted black olives, drained

8 garlic cloves, peeled

1 cup fresh basil leaves

1 cup rolled oats (not quick oats, gluten-free if necessary)

1½ cups cooked lentils

¼ cup nutritional yeast flakes

1 tablespoon lemon juice

1 tablespoon Dijon mustard

1 teaspoon onion powder

¼ teaspoon sea salt or to taste

Directions

1. Preheat the oven to 375°F. Line a rimmed baking sheet with parchment paper or a silicone mat.

2. Combine the walnuts, olives, garlic, basil, and oats in a food processor and process until finely ground. Transfer to a large bowl.

3. Add the lentils, nutritional yeast, lemon juice, mustard, onion powder, and salt and mix thoroughly.

4. Form the mixture into 6 patties. Place on the lined baking sheet and bake for 20–30 minutes or until crispy around the edges. Serve on a bun or in a wrap with lettuce, tomato, and toppings of your choice.

Tips & Hints

Most grocery stores do not carry canned lentils. To cook the lentils for this recipe, put ¾ cup dried lentils in a small saucepan and cover with water. Cover and cook over medium-low heat for 25–30 minutes or until tender, then drain.

Baked Spinach Quesadillas

Get ready for an easy Mexican-style grilled cheese sandwich from the oven! These fun quesadillas can be built quickly, and the entire batch cooks all at once so they are done at the same time. You can add more of your favorite veggie fillings along with the spinach and onion for extra flavor, texture, and heartiness—try corn or chopped bell peppers, mushrooms, or broccoli.

Prep Time: 15 minutes | Cook Time: 15 minutes | Yield: 4–6 servings

Ingredients

2 tablespoons lime juice

½ teaspoon chili powder

½ cup raw cashews

1½ cups unsweetened plant-based milk

1 tablespoon miso paste

5 tablespoons tapioca starch

2 tablespoons nutritional yeast flakes

1 teaspoon lemon juice

½ teaspoon garlic powder

½ teaspoon onion powder

¼ teaspoon sea salt or to taste

8 ounces spinach, chopped (about 4 cups)

1 cup finely diced red onion

4–6 large whole-grain or gluten-free tortillas

Shredded lettuce, salsa, and guacamole, for serving

Directions

1. Preheat the oven to 400°F. Line a rimmed baking sheet with parchment paper or a silicone mat.

2. In a small bowl, whisk together the lime juice and chili powder and set aside.

3. Combine the cashews, milk, miso paste, tapioca starch, nutritional yeast, lemon juice, garlic powder, onion powder, and salt in a high-powered blender. Blend until smooth and creamy.

4. Transfer the "cheese" sauce to a small saucepan and whisk over medium heat. At first it will appear lumpy, but continue cooking for about 5 minutes, until it is thickened, smooth, and stretchy.

5. Fold the spinach and onion into the cheese sauce until completely combined.

6. Spread the cheesy spinach mixture on half of each tortilla. Fold each tortilla over and place on the lined baking sheet. Brush the top of each quesadilla with the lime juice and chili powder

mixture. Bake for 6–8 minutes, turning once, until golden brown on both sides.

7. Serve warm with lettuce, salsa, and guacamole.

Tips & Hints

There is no substitution for tapioca starch in this recipe! That's what gives the cheese sauce its thick, stretchy consistency.

Appetizers and Dips

Chinese-Style Vegan Dumplings

These classic dumplings are easy and fun to create at home so you don't have to order take-out from a restaurant. And they taste so much better than any store-bought pot stickers. They're loaded with fresh veggies and wrapped in wonton wrappers, then steamed or baked to perfection. Dip these little gems into hoisin dipping sauce, and they are nothing short of perfection.

Prep Time: 30–45 minutes | Cook Time: 5–15 minutes | Yield: 30 dumplings

Ingredients

- 2 tablespoons low-sodium tamari or soy sauce
- 2 teaspoons grated ginger or ginger paste
- 2 teaspoons pure maple syrup (or other liquid sweetener)
- 2½ teaspoons cornstarch, plus more for dusting
- 1 carrot, grated
- 3 cups shredded napa cabbage or regular green cabbage
- 8 ounces mushrooms (any type), chopped
- 1 cup chopped green onions
- 1 (12-ounce) package vegan wonton wrappers (round or square)
- Cabbage leaves (optional, for steaming)
- Hoisin Dipping Sauce (page 134), for serving

Directions

1. In a small bowl, whisk together the tamari or soy sauce, ginger, maple syrup, and cornstarch until the lumps are gone. Set aside.

2. In a large skillet, sauté the carrot, cabbage, mushrooms, and green onions in a small amount of water over medium heat. When the vegetables begin to wilt and soften, add the cornstarch mixture and mix well. When the sauce starts to bubble and thicken, turn off the heat and set aside.

3. To stuff the dumplings, set a small bowl of water on a work surface beside the wonton wrappers and vegetable filling and dust a rimmed baking sheet with cornstarch. Take one wonton wrapper at a time and use your finger to moisten the edges. Drop about 1 tablespoon of vegetable filling in the center of each wrapper. Bring the sides of the wrapper up over the filling and press together to seal. If the wrapper doesn't seal, moisten the edges with a little more water. Pinch along the seam to create a decorative edge. Set each dumpling on the cornstarch-dusted baking sheet. Repeat until all the dumplings are made.

4. To cook the dumplings, you have a choice of methods:

    - **Steamer:** Pour 1–2 inches of water into a large pot and bring to a boil. Line a steamer basket or bamboo steamer with parchment paper or cabbage leaves. Place the dumplings in the steamer, cover, and steam for 7–8 minutes.

    - **Oven:** Arrange the dumplings in a single layer on a rimmed baking sheet lined with parchment paper or a silicone mat. Bake at 400°F for 10–15 minutes or until the edges are golden brown.

    - **Air fryer:** Place the dumplings in a single layer in the air fryer basket and air-fry at 400°F for 8 minutes or until the edges are golden brown and crispy.

    - **Boiling water:** Bring a large pot of water to a boil and add the dumplings. Stir so they don't stick together and cook for 2–3 minutes. Remove and rinse in warm water before serving. (This method requires extra-careful sealing of the dumpling edges so the filling doesn't get soggy.)

5. Serve the dumplings warm with the Hoisin Dipping Sauce.

Tips & Hints

These dumplings can be made ahead of time and stored in the refrigerator or freezer either cooked or uncooked.

Baked Corn Tortilla Chips

Crunchy tortilla chips are full of flavor and easy to make. You can serve these for taco night as a snack or dip them into your favorite plant-based cheese sauce, guacamole, or salsa.

Prep Time: 5 minutes | **Cook Time: 6–8 minutes** | **Yield: 2–3 servings**

Ingredients

2 tablespoons lime juice

2 tablespoons water

2 teaspoons chili powder

1 teaspoon sriracha

4–6 (6-inch) corn tortillas

Sea salt to taste

Directions

1. Preheat the oven to 350°F. Line a rimmed baking sheet with parchment paper or a silicone mat.

2. In a small bowl, whisk together the lime juice, water, chili powder, and sriracha. Brush each tortilla on both sides with the lime juice mixture and salt to taste. Cut each tortilla into 8 wedges and arrange the wedges on the lined baking sheet.

3. Bake for 6–8 minutes or until crispy and golden around the edges. Keep an eye on the tortilla chips toward the end of the time as they can burn very quickly.

Baked Thai Spring Rolls

These crispy baked spring rolls are loaded with delicious Thai-style veggies and rice noodles. Dip them into a sweet and spicy peanut sauce for the perfect party appetizer.

Prep Time: 25 minutes | Cook Time: 30 minutes | Yield: 4–6 servings

Ingredients

Stir-Fry Sauce

¼ cup water

3 tablespoons low-sodium tamari or soy sauce

2 tablespoons pure maple syrup (or other liquid sweetener)

1 tablespoon grated ginger or ginger paste

1 tablespoon rice vinegar

1 tablespoon lime juice

1 tablespoon cornstarch

1 teaspoon sriracha

1 teaspoon garlic powder

Spring Rolls

2 ounces bean thread rice noodles

2 cups Butler Soy Curls or 6 ounces mushrooms (any type), sliced

4 cups thinly sliced green cabbage

2 small carrots, julienned

4 green onions, thinly sliced

12–14 rice paper spring roll wrappers or frozen flour spring roll wrappers

Peanut Dipping Sauce

¼ cup all-natural peanut butter (100 percent peanuts)

1–3 tablespoons water

2 tablespoons low-sodium tamari or soy sauce

1 tablespoon lime juice

2 teaspoons pure maple syrup (or other liquid sweetener)

1½ teaspoons sriracha

1 teaspoon garlic powder

Directions

1. Preheat the oven to 425°F. Line a rimmed baking sheet with parchment paper or a silicone mat.

2. In a small bowl, whisk together all the stir-fry sauce ingredients; set aside.

3. Cook the rice noodles according to the package instructions; drain. Using kitchen shears, cut the noodles into 1–2-inch pieces. Set aside.

4. Put the Soy Curls (if using) in a bowl and cover with warm water. Soak for 10 minutes or until fully rehydrated. Drain.

5. Sauté the cabbage, carrots, green onions, and Soy Curls or mushrooms in a large skillet in a small amount of water over medium-high heat until the vegetables are tender, 6–8 minutes.

6. Add the stir-fry sauce and noodles and continue cooking until bubbly and thickened, 1–2 minutes. Remove from the heat.

7. Soak a rice paper wrapper in a bowl of warm water for 10 seconds or until it is pliable. (If you are using frozen flour spring roll wrappers, you do not need to soak the wrappers.) Place the wrapper on a work surface and add 2–3 tablespoons of the vegetable-noodle mixture to the lower half of the wrapper. Fold the left and right sides toward the middle and begin rolling as if you are making a burrito. Be careful not to overfill. Practice makes perfect! Repeat to fill all the rolls.

8. Arrange the spring rolls seam side down on the lined baking sheet and bake for 20–25 minutes or until lightly browned. For crispier spring rolls, turn them over halfway through baking.

9. While the spring rolls are baking, whisk together all the peanut dipping sauce ingredients in a small bowl.

10. Serve the baked spring rolls warm with the peanut dipping sauce.

Tips & Hints

Try changing up the filling by adding your favorite stir-fry veggies (such as bell peppers, mushrooms, or green onions) or baked tofu.

You don't have to bake these spring rolls! Just enjoy them soft and fresh right after rolling.

"Cheesy" Jalapeño Poppers

Stuffed jalapeño poppers never tasted so good! These creamy, smoky, and slightly spicy mini peppers will have you reaching for more. Once you prepare the delicious plant-based cheesy filling, you can quickly fill your sweet or spicy peppers and bake. These are the perfect appetizers for any occasion.

Prep Time: 30 minutes | Cook Time: 10–15 minutes | Yield: 8–10 servings

Ingredients

- 1 (15-ounce) can chickpeas, drained and rinsed
- 1 (14-ounce) package extra-firm tofu
- ½ cup nutritional yeast flakes
- 3 garlic cloves, peeled
- 3 tablespoons apple cider vinegar
- 2 tablespoons white miso paste
- 2 teaspoons onion powder
- 1 teaspoon smoked paprika, divided
- 12–14 jalapeño peppers or mini sweet peppers, halved, seeded, and ribs removed
- ¼ cup panko-style or gluten-free bread crumbs (optional)

Directions

1. Preheat the oven to 425°F. Line a rimmed baking sheet with parchment paper or a silicone mat.

2. In a food processor, combine the chickpeas, tofu, nutritional yeast, garlic, vinegar, miso paste, onion powder, and ½ teaspoon of the smoked paprika. Blend until smooth and creamy.

3. Evenly fill the pepper halves with the creamy mixture. Top the peppers with the panko (if using) and remaining ½ teaspoon smoked paprika.

4. Place the stuffed peppers on the lined baking sheet and bake for 10–15 minutes or until golden brown. Serve warm.

Tips & Hints

You may want to wear gloves when preparing this recipe as the capsicum oils from the jalapeño peppers can cause burning on the skin, especially if you rub or touch your eyes or face.

If you have any leftover filling, refrigerate it in an airtight container for up to 6 days. It makes a perfect sandwich spread or veggie dip.

Eggplant Caponata

When eggplants are in season, what better way to use them than in caponata? Caponata is a sweet-and-sour Italian dish that typically combines eggplant, onions, peppers, tomatoes, garlic, and a blend of herbs. I love every variety of olives in almost any dish, so I always add some extra olives. Enjoy caponata as a dip, tossed in pasta, or on top of whole-grain toast or polenta.

Prep Time: 20 minutes | Cook Time: 40 minutes | Yield: 4–6 servings

Ingredients

- 1½ pounds eggplant (1 large), cut into ¾-inch cubes
- 1 red onion, diced
- ¼ teaspoon red pepper flakes
- 8 garlic cloves, chopped
- 2 celery stalks, diced
- 1 red bell pepper, seeded and diced
- 1 (15-ounce) can diced tomatoes
- 3 tablespoons tomato paste
- ½ cup golden raisins
- ½ cup coarsely chopped green olives
- ½ cup coarsely chopped black olives
- 2 tablespoons capers, drained and rinsed
- ¼ cup red wine vinegar
- ¾ teaspoon sea salt or to taste
- ¼ teaspoon black pepper
- 2–3 tablespoons pine nuts (optional)
- ¼ cup chopped fresh mint

Directions

1. Preheat the oven to 425°F. Line a rimmed baking sheet with parchment paper or a silicone mat.

2. Spread out the diced eggplant in a single layer on the lined baking sheet. Bake for 15–20 minutes or until golden and tender.

3. Sauté the onion and red pepper flakes in a large skillet in a small amount of water over medium-high heat until tender. Add the garlic, celery, and bell pepper and cook, adding more water as needed, until the vegetables are tender.

4. Add the eggplant, tomatoes with their juices, tomato paste, raisins, olives, capers, vinegar, salt, and pepper and simmer over low heat for 20–30 minutes or until the mixture reduces and thickens.

5. Allow to cool and serve at room temperature, or chill and serve later. Just before serving, top with the pine nuts (if using) and mint.

Vegan Party Fondue GF

Pull out your skewers because it's time for fondue! Who knew healthy could be this good? It's difficult to figure out what *not* to dip in this creamy, cheesy sauce. Cashews and potatoes create a creamy foundation, which is perfectly seasoned with just the right balance of sour and salty. Fondue is romantic, social, and just plain fun—I hope this recipe inspires you to throw a party.

Prep Time: 15 minutes | **Cook Time: 15–20 minutes** | **Yield: 4–6 servings**

Ingredients

2 Yukon Gold potatoes (8–10 ounces), peeled and diced

1 yellow or white onion, quartered

½ cup raw cashews

4 garlic cloves

1½ cups unsweetened plant-based milk

1 cup unsweetened plant-based yogurt, store-bought (such as Kite Hill) or homemade (page 36)

½ cup dry white wine

2 tablespoons white miso paste

1 tablespoon white wine vinegar

1 tablespoon lemon juice

6 tablespoons nutritional yeast flakes

5 tablespoons tapioca starch

¾ teaspoon sea salt or to taste

½ teaspoon ground mustard

Whole-grain bread (gluten-free if necessary), roasted potatoes, roasted mushrooms, baked French fries, cut-up veggies, cherry tomatoes, and/or sliced apples, for dipping

Directions

1. Put the potatoes, onion, and cashews in a small saucepan and cover with water. Bring to a boil, then reduce the heat to medium-low. Cook just until the potatoes are tender, 10–15 minutes. Drain and allow to cool slightly.

2. Transfer the potatoes, onion, and cashews to a high-powered blender. Add the garlic, milk, yogurt, wine, miso paste, vinegar, lemon juice, nutritional yeast, tapioca starch, salt, and mustard and blend until smooth and creamy.

3. Pour the mixture into a large saucepan and whisk over medium-high heat until thick and bubbly. It will appear to get lumpy at first, but it will become evenly thickened after 4–5 minutes.

4. Pour the "cheese" mixture into a fondue pot or a small slow cooker and heat on low to keep it warm. Serve with your favorite dippers.

Loaded Nachos with BBQ Jackfruit

Loaded nachos are the ultimate game-day appetizer for sharing with family and friends. These crispy oil-free corn tortillas are piled high with BBQ jackfruit, vegan nacho sauce, and of course, an assortment of veggie toppings. You can customize this recipe with all the toppings your family loves.

Prep Time: 30 minutes | Cook Time: 30 minutes | Yield: 4 servings

Baked Tortillas

2 tablespoons lime juice (optional)

1 teaspoon chili powder (optional)

Sea salt to taste (optional)

12 (6-inch) corn tortillas, cut into 8 wedges

BBQ Jackfruit

2 (20-ounce) cans young green jackfruit in water, drained

1 small onion, diced

1 poblano pepper, seeded and diced

1 cup oil-free barbecue sauce (such as Bone Suckin' Sauce)

Vegan Nacho Sauce

½ cup raw cashews or raw sunflower seeds

1½ cups water

2 teaspoons lemon juice

2 garlic cloves, peeled

2 tablespoons nutritional yeast flakes

1½ teaspoons cornstarch

1 teaspoon smoked paprika

1 teaspoon onion powder

½ teaspoon sea salt or to taste

½ teaspoon ground cumin

¼ teaspoon chipotle chile powder, or more to taste

1 (4-ounce) can chopped green chiles, drained

Toppings (optional)

1–2 jalapeño peppers, thinly sliced, seeds and ribs removed if desired

1 avocado, pitted, peeled, and diced

1 red onion, finely diced

½ cup chopped fresh cilantro

1 cup salsa

2–3 limes, sliced

Directions

1. Preheat the oven to 350°F. Line a rimmed baking sheet with parchment paper or a silicone mat.

2. If desired, in a small bowl, whisk together the lime juice, chili powder, and salt. Brush each tortilla on both sides with the mixture. Cut each tortilla into 8 wedges and arrange the wedges on the lined baking sheet. Bake for 6–8 minutes or until crispy and slightly golden around the edges. Keep an eye on the tortilla chips toward the end of the time as they can burn very quickly.

3. Prepare the jackfruit by shredding the pieces with your hands. Then chop any hard pieces into small bits.

4. In a large skillet, sauté the onion and poblano pepper in a small amount of water over medium-high heat until tender. Add the shredded jackfruit and barbecue sauce, turn the heat down to low, and cook for 20 minutes. Add a bit of water if the mixture begins to dry out.

5. Meanwhile, combine the cashews, water, lemon juice, garlic, nutritional yeast, cornstarch, smoked paprika, onion powder, salt, cumin, and chipotle powder in a high-powered blender and blend on high until creamy and smooth. Transfer the mixture to a small saucepan and add the green chiles. Cook over medium-high heat for 3–5 minutes until bubbly and thickened.

6. To serve, scatter the tortilla chips on a large platter, pour the nacho sauce over them, and spoon on the BBQ jackfruit. Top with all your favorite nacho toppings.

Tips & Hints

You can add many other toppings to these nachos—some of our favorites are corn, sliced green onions, vegan sour cream or yogurt, black beans, pinto beans, pickled jalapeños, sliced black olives, and guacamole.

Muhammara

Simple quinoa flatbread (page 85) pairs beautifully with this roasted pepper and walnut spread, which is perfect as a dip or in sandwiches and wraps. The special ingredients in this bright and vibrant Middle Eastern recipe are the roasted red peppers and sweet and tangy pomegranate molasses. It's easy, festive, flavorful, and unique. Move over, hummus!

Prep Time: 15 minutes | Yield: 4 servings

Ingredients

3 red bell peppers, roasted, *or* 1 (16-ounce) jar roasted red peppers, drained

1 cup walnuts, toasted

2 garlic cloves, peeled

½ cup whole-grain bread crumbs (gluten-free if necessary)

2 tablespoons pomegranate molasses

1 tablespoon tomato paste

1 tablespoon lemon juice

1 teaspoon smoked paprika

½ teaspoon red pepper flakes

½ teaspoon ground cumin

½ teaspoon sea salt or to taste

Directions

Combine all the ingredients in a food processor and blend on high until a smooth, even consistency is achieved.

Tips & Hints

To roast bell peppers, place the whole peppers on a rimmed baking sheet. Roast at 450°F for 20–25 minutes or until blackened on the outside. Remove from the oven and set aside to cool in a covered bowl or a paper bag. Slice the cooled peppers in half and peel away the skin, seeds, and ribs.

To toast walnuts, evenly spread walnuts on a parchment-lined baking sheet and place in the oven at 375°F for 5–10 minutes or just until they start to brown and smell toasted. Watch them carefully as walnuts will burn very quickly.

If you cannot locate pomegranate molasses, you can substitute a mixture of 1 tablespoon pure maple syrup and 1 tablespoon balsamic vinegar.

Savory Corn Fritters

Corn fritters are a cross between a pancake and a cookie. Traditionally, corn fritters are southern-deep-fried, but this recipe is oil-free. It features savory Mexican flavors combined with fresh peppers, onion, corn, and cilantro. Corn fritters are the perfect accompaniment to chili, Mexican salad, or rice and beans, or they can be served on their own, topped with vegan yogurt, fresh cilantro, and sliced avocado.

Prep Time: 20 minutes | **Cook Time: 15 minutes** | **Yield: 4 servings**

Ingredients

Veggies

2 cups fresh or (thawed) frozen corn kernels

1 poblano pepper, seeded and small diced

1 red bell pepper, seeded and small diced

¼ cup finely chopped red onion

¼ cup chopped fresh cilantro

Batter

1 cup unsweetened plant-based milk

½ cup oat flour

½ cup chickpea flour

¼ cup finely ground cornmeal

1 tablespoon grated lime zest

2 teaspoons chili powder

½ teaspoon baking powder

½ teaspoon onion powder

½ teaspoon garlic powder

½ teaspoon ground cumin

½ teaspoon sea salt or to taste

¼ teaspoon black pepper

¼ teaspoon ground turmeric

Directions

1. Preheat the oven to 400°F. Line a rimmed baking sheet with parchment paper or a silicone mat.

2. In a medium bowl, toss together all the veggies. In another medium bowl, whisk together all the batter ingredients. Fold the veggies into the batter and mix well.

3. Drop large spoonfuls of the fritter mixture onto the lined baking sheet and flatten with the back of a wet spoon.

4. Bake for 6–8 minutes on each side or until the fritters turn a beautiful golden color. Serve warm.

Spinach Artichoke Dip

This cheesy dip makes the perfect party dish, served with bread, chips, or veggies. We also like to use it as a sandwich filling and as a topping for baked potatoes or pasta with grilled veggies. The possibilities are endless!

Prep Time: 20 minutes | Cook Time: 30 minutes | Yield: 6 servings

Ingredients

"Cheese" Sauce

½ cup raw cashews

1½ cups unsweetened plant-based milk

5 tablespoons tapioca starch

2 tablespoons nutritional yeast flakes

1–2 tablespoons miso paste

1 teaspoon lemon juice

½ teaspoon garlic powder

½ teaspoon onion powder

¼ teaspoon sea salt or to taste

Filling

1 cup canned or (thawed) frozen chopped artichoke hearts

½ cup red onion, finely diced

3 garlic cloves, minced

2 cups fresh or (thawed) frozen chopped spinach

¼ cup unsweetened plant-based milk

¼ teaspoon salt

¼ teaspoon black pepper

Directions

1. Preheat the oven to 400°F.

2. Combine all the cheese sauce ingredients in a medium saucepan. Whisk over medium heat until the sauce is thick and bubbly, about 5 minutes. It will appear to get lumpy, but it will eventually become evenly thickened and stretchy.

3. Add the artichoke hearts, onion, garlic, spinach, milk, salt, and pepper and fold into the cheese mixture until the ingredients are thoroughly combined.

4. Transfer the mixture to a small baking pan and bake for 20 minutes, stirring once halfway through.

5. Turn on the oven broiler. Broil for 3 minutes or until the top becomes golden brown.

Veggie Lover Sushi Rolls

Sushi is fun to create at home and even more enjoyable to eat! Once you learn the basic technique, you'll want to add these little nutrition-packed rice rolls to your menu often. The ingredients are simple: seaweed, seasoned rice, and just about any fresh vegetables. Feel free to substitute your own!

Prep Time: 30 minutes | Yield: 36 pieces

Ingredients

Rice

4 cups freshly cooked short-grain brown rice or white sushi rice (about 2 cups uncooked rice)

¼ cup rice vinegar

2 tablespoons pure maple syrup (or other liquid sweetener)

½ teaspoon sea salt or to taste

Sushi

6 nori sheets

¼ cup sesame seeds

1 red bell pepper, seeded and thinly sliced

2 carrots, shredded

1 small cucumber, thinly sliced

2 cups finely chopped spinach or kale

1 avocado, pitted, peeled, and sliced

For Serving (optional)

Pickled ginger

Low-sodium tamari or soy sauce

Wasabi powder or paste

Directions

1. Put the hot rice in a large bowl and gently fold in the rice vinegar, maple syrup, and salt.

2. To make uramaki-style sushi (rice on the outside), cover a sushi mat with plastic wrap. Cut a nori sheet in half. Lay the nori sheet on the sushi mat with the rough side facing up. Using wet fingers or a spatula, spread ½–¾ cup of the warm rice evenly over the nori sheet, leaving about ¼ inch uncovered at the bottom edge of the sheet and pushing the rice to the outer edges. Sprinkle the rice with ½–1 tablespoon of the sesame seeds. Carefully pick up the nori sheet and flip the rice-covered nori over so the rice is facing down.

3. Arrange a generous serving of veggies in a line on the bottom three-quarters of the nori sheet closest to you. Start rolling away from you, using your mat to keep the roll in place. Apply some pressure to make a tight roll. (If it's not tight enough, it will be difficult to cut.) Once the veggies are covered, roll the mat over to mold and compress the roll. Continue until it's rolled up all the way. Allow the roll to rest for 5 minutes, then fill and roll the remaining nori sheets.

4. Using a very sharp serrated knife, cut each sushi roll into 6 equal pieces. Run your knife through a damp cloth before every slice so the rice won't stick.

5. To make maki-style sushi (rice on the inside), lay a whole nori sheet on a sushi mat with the rough side facing up. Using wet fingers or a spatula, spread about ¾ cup of the warm rice evenly over the nori sheet, pushing the rice to the outer edges.

6. Arrange a generous serving of veggies in a line on the bottom three-quarters of the rice closest to you. Begin to roll the rice over with your fingers, and once the veggies are covered, roll the mat over to mold and compress the roll. Continue until it's rolled up all the way. Allow the roll to rest for 5 minutes, then fill and roll the remaining nori sheets.

7. Using a very sharp serrated knife, cut each sushi roll in half, then line the two halves up and slice into ½-inch-thick rings. Run your knife through a damp cloth before every slice so the rice won't stick. Garnish with sesame seeds.

8. Serve immediately with pickled ginger, tamari or soy sauce, and wasabi, if you like.

Tips & Hints

Try changing up the vegetable filling with baked tofu, sprouts, beets, mangoes, roasted sweet potatoes, or roasted shitake mushrooms.

Zucchini Poppers

Zucchini poppers make flavorful and healthy appetizers, and they are a great way to use up the zucchini from your summer garden. Zucchini doesn't have a lot of flavor alone but absorbs added flavors beautifully. These appetizers have a mild cheesy flavor that both kids and adults love. Eat them on their own or in a sandwich or wrap.

Prep Time: 15 minutes | **Cook Time: 15–18 minutes** | **Yield: 4 servings**

Ingredients

- 4 cups shredded zucchini
- 1 onion, grated
- 1½ cup whole-grain bread crumbs (gluten-free if necessary) (about 3–4 slices whole-grain bread, finely ground)
- ½ cup nutritional yeast flakes
- 2 tablespoons cornstarch
- 2 tablespoons tahini
- 1 tablespoon white miso paste
- 1 teaspoon onion powder
- 1 teaspoon garlic powder

Directions

1. Preheat the oven to 400°F. Line a rimmed baking sheet with parchment paper or a silicone mat.

2. Wrap the zucchini in a clean towel and squeeze out any excess water.

3. In a medium bowl, combine the zucchini, onion, bread crumbs, nutritional yeast, cornstarch, tahini, miso paste, onion powder, and garlic powder and mix well.

4. Roll 1–2 tablespoons of the mixture into a small cylinder and place on the lined baking sheet. Repeat with the rest of the mixture. Bake for 15–18 minutes or until golden brown, crispy, and dry to the touch. Serve warm.

Tips & Hints

You can shape these poppers into patties, balls, or even mini muffins. These freeze great, so double the recipe and fill your freezer!

Dressings and Sauces

Mint Yogurt Chutney (page 132)

Creamy Cranberry
Dressing (page 130)

Cilantro Lime
Dressing (page 133)

Sweet Mustard
Dressing (page 130)

Tofu Cashew
Mayonnaise (page 131)

Poppy Seed Dressing
(page 129)

Poppy Seed Dressing GF

This tangy-sweet creamy dressing is perfect for any salad or as a dipping sauce for fresh veggies. It's simple to make and ready in seconds. I love this dressing on a spinach salad topped with fresh strawberries.

Prep Time: 5 minutes | **Yield: 1¼ cups**

Ingredients

½ cup unsweetened plant-based milk

2½ tablespoons sunflower seeds

2 tablespoons water

2 tablespoons apple cider vinegar

2 tablespoons pure maple syrup (or other liquid sweetener)

1 tablespoon lemon juice

2 teaspoons onion powder

1 teaspoon Dijon mustard

½ teaspoon garlic powder

½ teaspoon sea salt or to taste

1 tablespoon poppy seeds

Directions

Combine the milk, sunflower seeds, water, vinegar, maple syrup, lemon juice, onion powder, mustard, garlic powder, and salt in a high-powered blender and blend for 30–60 seconds or until smooth. Add the poppy seeds and pulse 3 or 4 times or until thoroughly combined. The dressing will continue to thicken when refrigerated. Store in an airtight container in the refrigerator for up to 1 week.

Creamy Cranberry Dressing

This vibrant and colorful cranberry dressing is perfect for dressing up holiday salads. It's a simple and fun recipe with the addition of colorful zesty cranberries. Just throw it all in a blender and let the magic begin!

Prep Time: 10 minutes | Yield: 1 cup

Ingredients

1 cup fresh cranberries

2 ounces extra-firm tofu, drained

¼ cup water, or more if you prefer a thinner consistency

1 garlic clove, peeled

1 tablespoon white miso paste

1 tablespoon red wine vinegar

1 tablespoon pure maple syrup (or other liquid sweetener)

1 teaspoon Dijon mustard

1 tablespoon fresh thyme *or* ½ teaspoon dried thyme

¼ teaspoon sea salt or to taste

Directions

Combine all the ingredients in a blender and blend until smooth and creamy. Store in an airtight container in the refrigerator for up to 5 days.

Sweet Mustard Dressing

This dressing is a delicious replacement for traditional honey mustard dressing. It's smooth and creamy, with perfectly balanced flavors.

Prep Time: 5 minutes | Yield: 1½ cups

Ingredients

4 ounces extra-firm tofu, drained

5 pitted dates, soaked

¾ cup water

¼ cup yellow mustard

2 tablespoons apple cider vinegar

1 tablespoon lemon juice

Directions

Combine all the ingredients in a blender and blend until smooth and creamy. Store in an airtight container in the refrigerator for 5–7 days.

Tofu Cashew Mayonnaise

This plant-based mayonnaise is so rich and full of flavor that you will not miss your old egg-and-oil-based mayonnaise. I like to make a batch every week or two to have on hand for sandwiches, dressings, and sauces.

Prep Time: 10 minutes | Yield: 1¼ cups

Ingredients

7 ounces extra-firm tofu, drained

¼ cup raw cashews (optional)

2 tablespoons apple cider vinegar

1–2 tablespoons water

1 tablespoon lemon juice

2 teaspoons pure maple syrup (or other liquid sweetener)

1 teaspoon Dijon mustard

½ teaspoon sea salt or to taste

Directions

Combine all the ingredients in a blender (a high-powered blender works best if you're using the cashews) and blend until smooth and shiny. Store in an airtight container in the refrigerator for 5–7 days.

Hollandaise Sauce

A typical hollandaise sauce is heavy with egg yolks and butter. This mild and creamy cashew-based version goes nicely on almost any vegetable. We love it over asparagus with toast or polenta.

Prep Time: 10 minutes | Yield: 1 cup (4 servings)

Ingredients

¾ cup unsweetened plant-based milk

½ cup raw cashews

2 garlic cloves, peeled

2 tablespoons lemon juice

2 tablespoons nutritional yeast flakes

1 tablespoon onion powder

½ teaspoon ground mustard

¼ teaspoon ground turmeric

¼ teaspoon sea salt or to taste

⅛ teaspoon cayenne pepper (optional)

Directions

Combine all the ingredients in a high-powered blender and blend until smooth and creamy. Store in an airtight container in the refrigerator for 5–7 days.

Mint Yogurt Chutney

This condiment pairs perfectly with your favorite curries and other Indian dishes. It's an ideal balance of sweet, sour, and spicy.

Prep Time: 10 minutes | Yield: 1¼ cups

Ingredients

1 cup unsweetened plant-based yogurt, store-bought (such as Kite Hill) or homemade (page 36)

½ cup fresh cilantro leaves

¼ cup fresh mint leaves

2 garlic cloves, peeled

1 jalapeño pepper, seeded

1 tablespoon lime juice

2 teaspoons grated ginger or ginger paste

2 teaspoons pure maple syrup (or other liquid sweetener) or to taste

¼ teaspoon sea salt or to taste

Directions

Combine all the ingredients in a blender and blend until smooth and creamy. Store in an airtight container in the refrigerator for up to 3 days.

Cilantro Lime Dressing

This fresh dressing is perfect on any hearty Mexican salad. It's sweet and creamy with the perfect amount of spice.

Prep Time: 10 minutes | Yield: 1¼ cups

Ingredients

½ cup orange juice

¼ cup water, or more if you prefer a thinner consistency

2 tablespoons lime juice

2 tablespoons apple cider vinegar

1 tablespoon pure maple syrup (or other liquid sweetener)

2 garlic cloves, peeled

1 large ripe avocado, pitted and peeled

½ cup fresh cilantro leaves

1 jalapeño pepper, seeded

¼ teaspoon ground cumin

¼ teaspoon sea salt or to taste

Directions

Combine all the ingredients in a blender and blend until creamy. Store in an airtight container in the refrigerator for up to 5 days.

Lemon Tahini Dressing

This creamy oil-free dressing is a flavor powerhouse. It's smooth, rich, nutty, tangy—and perfect as a salad dressing, a dip, or a topping for your favorite vegan falafel or burger.

Prep Time: 5 minutes | Yield: 1 cup

Ingredients

½ cup water

¼ cup tahini

¼ cup lemon juice

2 pitted dates, soaked

2 garlic cloves, peeled

¼ cup fresh cilantro leaves

¼ cup fresh flat-leaf parsley leaves

½ teaspoon sea salt or to taste

Directions

Combine all the ingredients in a blender and blend until smooth and creamy. Store in an airtight container in the refrigerator for 5–7 days.

Hoisin Dipping Sauce /GF

Hoisin is a thick, flavorful sauce that is used to season many Chinese dishes. It is quite salty and sweet, so a little can go a long way. Most recipes call for a small amount of hoisin sauce to enhance the dish. This sauce is oil-free and can be made gluten-free by using tamari instead of soy sauce.

Prep Time: 5 minutes | Yield: ½ cup (4 servings)

Ingredients

3 tablespoons low-sodium tamari

2 tablespoons all-natural peanut butter (100 percent peanuts)

2 tablespoons pure maple syrup (or other liquid sweetener)

1 tablespoon molasses

1 tablespoon rice vinegar

1 teaspoon sriracha

½ teaspoon garlic powder

½ teaspoon onion powder

¼ teaspoon Chinese five-spice powder, store-bought or homemade (page 68)

Directions

Combine all the ingredients in a bowl and whisk until everything is well incorporated. Store in an airtight container in the refrigerator for 5–7 days.

Salads and Side Dishes

Brussels Sprout Salad

Brussels sprouts make the perfect cool-weather crunchy salad, with a texture more like a slaw. This autumn salad pairs the flavors of smoky bac'n chickpeas with a sweet, creamy dressing. If you've given up on the strong flavor of cooked Brussels sprouts, give them a try raw because the flavor is mild yet unique.

Prep Time: 20 minutes | Cook Time: 15–20 minutes | Yield: 4 servings

Ingredients

Bac'n Chickpeas

3 tablespoons low-sodium tamari

6 tablespoons nutritional yeast flakes

1 teaspoon pure maple syrup (or other liquid sweetener)

½ teaspoon liquid smoke

1 (15-ounce) can chickpeas, drained and rinsed

Dressing

3 tablespoons sunflower seeds

3 tablespoons red wine vinegar

1 tablespoon Dijon mustard

1 tablespoon pure maple syrup (or other liquid sweetener)

1 garlic clove, peeled

½ cup water

¼ teaspoon sea salt or to taste

¼ teaspoon black pepper

Salad

1 pound Brussels sprouts, trimmed and shredded

½ cup chopped walnuts or pecans

½ cup small-diced red onion

1 small apple, cored and small diced

½ cup raisins or dried cranberries

1 avocado, pitted, peeled, and diced

1 cup cooked quinoa

Directions

1. Preheat the oven to 400°F. Line a rimmed baking sheet with parchment paper or a silicone mat.

2. In a medium bowl, whisk together the tamari or soy sauce, nutritional yeast, maple syrup, and liquid smoke. Add the chickpeas and mix to coat well.

3. Spread out the chickpeas on the lined baking sheet and bake for 15–20 minutes or until crispy around the edges. Turn off the oven and leave the chickpeas in the oven until you are ready to add them to the salad.

4. Combine all the dressing ingredients in a high-powered blender and blend until smooth and creamy.

5. In a large bowl, toss together the Brussels sprouts, nuts, onion, apple, raisins or cranberries, avocado, and quinoa.

6. Pour the dressing over the salad and toss until well coated. Top with the roasted bac'n chickpeas and serve.

Tips & Hints

In addition to making great salad toppers, these bac'n chickpeas are perfect for anything that calls for bacon bits. We also love them just for snacking!

Cranberry Orange Roasted Brussels Sprouts GF

Cranberry and orange is a tried-and-true flavor combination that pairs well with Brussels sprouts. Brussels sprouts are the perfect fall and winter vegetable for roasting, and this wonderfully sweet-and-sour holiday side dish is simple to make.

Prep Time: 15 minutes | Cook Time: 20–25 minutes | Yield: 4–6 servings

Ingredients

1 tablespoon grated orange zest

¼ cup orange juice

2 tablespoons balsamic vinegar

2 tablespoons pure maple syrup (or other liquid sweetener)

1 tablespoon grated ginger or ginger paste

2 teaspoons Dijon mustard

¼ teaspoon sea salt or to taste

¼ teaspoon black pepper

1 pound Brussels sprouts, trimmed and halved

¼ cup minced shallots

8 ounces fresh cranberries

Directions

1. Preheat the oven to 400°F. Line a rimmed baking sheet with parchment paper or a silicone mat.

2. In a large bowl, whisk together the orange zest and juice, vinegar, maple syrup, ginger, mustard, salt, and pepper. Transfer 2 tablespoons of the sauce to a small bowl and set aside for the cranberries.

3. Add the Brussels sprouts and shallots to the large bowl and toss to coat with the sauce. Transfer the Brussels sprout mixture to the lined baking sheet and roast for 15 minutes or until golden brown and tender.

4. Meanwhile, toss the cranberries with the reserved sauce in the small bowl.

5. After the Brussels sprouts have roasted for 15 minutes, add the cranberries and roast for another 5–10 minutes or until the cranberries begin to soften and shrivel. Keep an eye on the cranberries as they can burn quickly. Serve immediately.

Marinated Carrot Salad

This traditional make-ahead sweet-and-sour salad is a favorite Thanksgiving side dish in our home. It's loaded with sliced carrots, bell peppers, onions, and celery, all smothered in a flavorful tomato-based sauce that is simple to prepare.

Prep Time: 15 minutes, plus 4 hours marinating time | Cook Time: 15 minutes | Yield: 4 servings

Ingredients

2 pounds carrots, sliced

1 cup tomato sauce

½ cup white vinegar

¼ cup pure maple syrup (or other liquid sweetener)

1 tablespoon Dijon mustard

1 tablespoon cornstarch

2 teaspoons vegan Worcestershire sauce

½ teaspoon sea salt or to taste

2 celery stalks, small diced

1 red onion, small diced

1 green bell pepper, seeded and small diced

4 garlic cloves, finely chopped

Directions

1. Bring a large pot of water to a boil, add the carrots, and simmer over medium heat until tender, 5–8 minutes. Do not overcook the carrots; they should be firm, not mushy. Drain and rinse the carrots in cold water. Set aside.

2. In a medium saucepan, whisk the tomato sauce, vinegar, maple syrup, mustard, cornstarch, Worcestershire sauce, and salt until there are no lumps. Turn the heat to medium-high and allow the mixture to become bubbly and thick. Turn off the heat and allow the mixture to cool.

3. Combine the carrots, celery, onion, bell pepper, and garlic in a large bowl and cover with the cooled tomato sauce mixture, tossing to coat. Cover and refrigerate for at least 4 hours to allow the carrots to marinate fully.

Raw Pad Thai Zoodles

Zucchini makes perfect raw noodles for a beautiful, unique, and fun salad. The peanut sauce is loaded with sweet, sour, and spicy flavors.

Prep Time: 30 minutes | **Yield: 4 servings**

Ingredients

Sauce

¼ cup all-natural peanut butter (100 percent peanuts)

3 tablespoons lime juice

3 tablespoons low-sodium tamari or soy sauce

2 tablespoons water

1 tablespoon rice vinegar

1 tablespoon pure maple syrup (or other liquid sweetener)

1–2 teaspoons sriracha

1 teaspoon grated ginger or ginger paste

1 teaspoon minced garlic

Vegetables

2 medium zucchini, spiralized

1 cup shredded or finely sliced red cabbage

1 red or yellow bell pepper, seeded and sliced

1 carrot, shredded

4–6 green onions, sliced

⅓ cup chopped fresh cilantro

⅓ cup chopped or whole peanuts

Directions

1. In a large bowl, whisk together all the sauce ingredients.

2. Add the zucchini, cabbage, bell pepper, carrot, green onions, and cilantro and toss well to coat. Top with the peanuts and serve.

Tips & Hints

If you enjoy making spiralized salads, you might like to invest in a good spiralizer. I've tried a few and had the most success with Paderno.

Chickpea Quinoa Salad

This dish is a protein-packed powerhouse! Enjoy the refreshing flavors of garlic, lemon, and tahini paired with a sweet, crunchy, and colorful vegetable base. It can be a meal by itself, a simple side, or a crowd-pleasing dish to share.

Prep Time: 15 minutes | **Yield: 4 servings**

Ingredients

Veggies

2 (15-ounce) cans chickpeas, drained and rinsed

2 cups cooked red quinoa

2 cups finely chopped kale

2 carrots, shredded

1 red bell pepper, seeded and diced

1 small red onion, finely diced

½ cup golden raisins

Dressing

½ cup lemon juice

¼ cup water

2 tablespoons tahini

1 tablespoon apple cider vinegar

1 tablespoon pure maple syrup (or other liquid sweetener)

2 garlic cloves, peeled

½ teaspoon sea salt or to taste

Directions

1. Combine all the veggies in a large bowl.

2. Blend all the dressing ingredients in a blender until smooth and creamy.

3. Pour the dressing over the veggies and toss gently. Cover and chill; serve cold.

Thai Fried Rice GF

This Thai-style dish is loaded with veggies, spices, and tofu for that perfect replication of traditional fried rice without oil or eggs. It's a perfect use for leftover rice—but sometimes I deliberately make a double batch of rice so I can whip up this easy and delicious dish the next day.

Prep Time: 20 minutes | Cook Time: 15 minutes | Yield: 4 servings

Ingredients

1 onion, diced

2 teaspoons grated ginger or ginger paste

4 garlic cloves, minced

¼ teaspoon ground turmeric

7 ounces extra-firm tofu, drained and crumbled

1½ cups fresh, canned, or (thawed) frozen diced pineapple

1 red bell pepper, seeded and small diced

1 carrot, small diced

¾ cup sliced green onions

1 cup fresh or (thawed) frozen peas

¼ cup low-sodium tamari or soy sauce

1 tablespoon pure maple syrup (or other liquid sweetener)

1 tablespoon lime juice

1–2 teaspoons sriracha

3 cups cooked and chilled brown rice

¼ cup chopped fresh cilantro

½ cup chopped peanuts

Lime wedges, for serving

Directions

1. In a large skillet, sauté the onion in a small amount of water over medium-high heat. Add the ginger, garlic, turmeric, and crumbled tofu and continue to sauté until well combined. Add the pineapple, bell pepper, carrot, green onions, and peas and stir-fry for 3–4 minutes, adding more water as needed.

2. Add the tamari or soy sauce, maple syrup, lime juice, and sriracha and mix well.

3. Add the cooked rice, turn the heat down to medium-low, and cook until the rice is heated through. Serve warm, topped with the cilantro and peanuts, with lime wedges on the side for squeezing.

Tips & Hints

Feel free to add or substitute your favorite seasonal veggies, such as corn, chopped kale, asparagus, tomatoes, broccoli, or cabbage.

Roasted Kabocha Squash with Sesame Ginger Sauce GF

Kabocha squash is a Japanese pumpkin with a beautiful orange flesh that tastes buttery, creamy, and slightly sweet. It's absolutely delicious! When roasted, this squash truly shines. The sweet and salty tang of the sesame ginger sauce highlights the kabocha flavor.

Prep Time: 15 minutes | Cook Time: 30–40 minutes | Yield: 4 servings

Ingredients

- 1 medium kabocha squash, seeded and cut into wedges
- 2 tablespoons sesame seeds, toasted
- 2 tablespoons low-sodium tamari or soy sauce
- 2 tablespoons lime juice
- 2 tablespoons water
- 1 tablespoon grated ginger or ginger paste
- 1 tablespoon pure maple syrup (or other liquid sweetener)
- 1 tablespoon tahini
- ½ teaspoon garlic powder

Directions

1. Preheat the oven to 375°F. Line a rimmed baking sheet with parchment paper or a silicone mat.

2. Place the squash wedges on the lined baking sheet.

3. Combine the sesame seeds, tamari or soy sauce, lime juice, water, ginger, maple syrup, tahini, and garlic powder in a blender and blend until just combined but not completely smooth.

4. Using a brush, coat the flesh of the kabocha squash with the sesame ginger sauce. (If you have leftover sauce, you can top the roasted squash with more sauce before serving.)

5. Bake for 30–40 minutes or until fork-tender.

Tips & Hints

You can eat the skin of the kabocha squash, so be sure to wash it well.

You can toast sesame seeds on a baking sheet at 375°F for 3–4 minutes or in a dry skillet over medium heat, stirring continuously, for 2–3 minutes. When golden and fragrant, remove them from the heat.

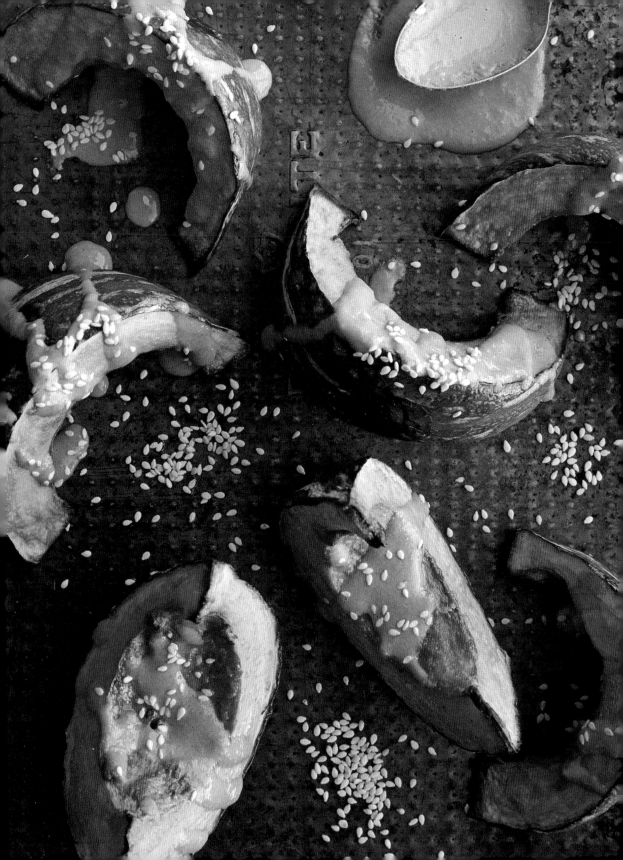

Entrées

Broccoli Chik'n Divan

Nothing says comfort food like a hot, creamy casserole loaded with broccoli, cauliflower, and Soy Curls. This easy and satisfying dinner recipe is sure to become a family favorite. Serve over your favorite rice or pasta.

Prep Time: 20 minutes | Cook Time: 35 minutes | Yield: 4–6 servings

Ingredients

Veggies

4 ounces Butler Soy Curls

1 pound broccoli, chopped

1 pound cauliflower, chopped

1 red onion, diced

Sauce

2½ cups unsweetened plant-based milk

½ cup raw cashews

¼ cup nutritional yeast flakes

3 garlic cloves, peeled

1 tablespoon cornstarch

1 tablespoon Dijon mustard

2 teaspoons lemon juice

½ teaspoon sea salt or to taste

½ teaspoon black pepper

Topping

½ cup whole-grain bread crumbs (gluten-free if necessary) (about 1 slice whole-grain bread, finely ground)

¼–½ cup chopped pecans or almonds

Directions

1. Preheat the oven to 375°F. Line a 9 × 13-inch baking pan with parchment paper.

2. Put the Soy Curls in a bowl and cover with warm water. Soak for 10 minutes or until fully rehydrated. Drain.

3. Meanwhile, in a steamer basket or microwave, steam the broccoli and cauliflower for 3–5 minutes or until tender-crisp.

4. Combine the Soy Curls, broccoli, cauliflower, and onion in the lined baking pan, spreading everything evenly.

5. Combine all the sauce ingredients in a high-powered blender and blend until smooth and creamy.

6. Pour the sauce over the vegetables, then top with the bread crumbs and nuts.

7. Cover the baking pan with aluminum foil and bake for 20 minutes. Remove the foil and continue baking for another 10 minutes or until the bread crumbs and nuts are golden brown and the sauce is bubbly. Serve warm.

Buffalo Potpie

If you miss the flavor of Buffalo chicken wings, you will love this potpie. It starts with sautéed veggies combined with Soy Curls and a creamy Buffalo-style sauce, is topped with slightly sweet cornbread, and baked to bubbly perfection. The flavors, colors, and textures make this dish comfort food for sure!

Prep Time: 20 minutes | Cook Time: 25 minutes | Yield: 4–6 servings

Ingredients

Veggies

4 ounces Butler Soy Curls

1 onion, diced

2 cups shredded carrots (about 4 medium carrots)

3 celery stalks, diced

4 garlic cloves, chopped

Sauce

2 cups unsweetened plant-based milk

¼ cup raw cashews

¼ cup hot sauce (such as Frank's RedHot)

2 tablespoons tahini

2 tablespoons apple cider vinegar

2 tablespoons nutritional yeast flakes

2 tablespoons cornstarch

1 teaspoon lemon juice

½ teaspoon sea salt or to taste

Cornbread

1 cup fine cornmeal

½ cup whole-wheat flour

1 teaspoon baking powder

¼ teaspoon baking soda

⅛ teaspoon sea salt

¾ cup unsweetened plant-based milk

¼ cup unsweetened applesauce

1 tablespoon pure maple syrup (or other liquid sweetener)

1½ teaspoons apple cider vinegar

Directions

1. Preheat the oven to 350°F.

2. Put the Soy Curls in a bowl and cover with warm water. Soak for 10 minutes or until fully rehydrated. Drain.

3. In a large skillet, sauté the onion in a small amount of water over medium-high heat until tender. Add the carrots, celery, and garlic and continue to cook for 3–5 minutes. Stir in the Soy Curls and remove from the heat.

4. Combine all the sauce ingredients in a high-powered blender and blend until smooth and creamy. Add the sauce to the skillet and mix well.

5. Transfer the mixture to a 9 × 13-inch baking pan, evenly spreading it out.

6. In a medium bowl, whisk together the cornmeal, flour, baking powder, baking soda, and salt. Add the milk, applesauce, maple syrup, and vinegar and mix just until the flour is moistened. Drop the cornbread batter by the spoonful on top of the casserole, covering it completely.

7. Bake for 20 minutes or until the cornbread is baked through and the top begins to brown. Serve warm.

Tips & Hints

I love to add peas, chopped spinach, or chopped kale to this recipe for color and added nutrients.

Cauliflower Walnut Tacos

Cauliflower and walnuts make a fantastic taco filling with great texture and flavor. You can also use this filling for salads, stuffed peppers, pizza, raw collard wraps, Mexican lasagna, and pasta.

Prep Time: 20 minutes | Cook Time: 30 minutes | Yield: 4–6 servings

Ingredients

Tacos

8 (6-inch) corn tortillas

1 pound cauliflower, cut into florets

1 cup walnuts

4 ounces mushrooms (any type) (optional)

1 onion, roughly chopped (optional)

1 tablespoon lime juice

2 tablespoons chili powder

1 teaspoon smoked paprika

1 teaspoon dried oregano

1 teaspoon garlic powder

1 teaspoon onion powder

½ teaspoon ground cumin

½ teaspoon sea salt or to taste

¼ teaspoon black pepper

Cilantro Lime Dressing

1 large ripe avocado, pitted and peeled

2 garlic cloves, peeled

1 jalapeño pepper, seeded

½ cup fresh cilantro leaves

½ cup orange juice

¼ cup water, or more as needed

2 tablespoons lime juice

2 tablespoons apple cider vinegar

1 tablespoon pure maple syrup (or other liquid sweetener)

¼ teaspoon ground cumin

¼ teaspoon sea salt or to taste

Toppings (optional)

2 cups mixed greens

1 cup sliced olives

1 cup sliced green or red bell peppers

½ cup sliced green onions

2 cups fresh or (thawed) frozen corn

1 mango, pitted, peeled, and diced

Directions

1. Preheat the oven to 400°F. Line a rimmed baking sheet with parchment paper or a silicone mat.

2. Wrap the tortillas in a slightly damp cloth or paper towel and microwave for 30 seconds. Drape each tortilla over two bars of an oven rack and bake for 8–10 minutes to crisp up into a taco shell shape. Watch the tortillas carefully as they can burn quickly. Remove and set aside.

3. Put the cauliflower, walnuts, mushrooms (if using), and onion (if using) in a food processor and process until the mixture looks like rice. Be careful not to puree the mixture.

4. Transfer the mixture to a large bowl, add the lime juice, chili powder, smoked paprika, oregano, garlic powder, onion powder, cumin, salt, and pepper and mix thoroughly. Spread out the mixture on the lined baking sheet and bake for 20–30 minutes or until the filling is golden brown and as dry as you like.

5. Meanwhile, combine all the dressing ingredients in a blender and blend until creamy and smooth.

6. Fill the taco shells with the cauliflower walnut filling, drizzle with the dressing, and add your choice of toppings.

Tips & Hints

It's easy to put together your own blend of Mexican spices, so don't be afraid to venture away from the recipe and substitute your own favorite mixture. (You can find my Homemade Taco Seasoning on page 66.) You can also use prepared taco seasoning.

Tips & Hints

This dish gains flavor the longer it sits, so it's the perfect meal to make ahead of time.

Try adding any combination of veggies to the sauce, such as cauliflower, peas, potatoes, and broccoli.

Chickpea Tikka Masala

This recipe is for every lover of Indian cuisine. Its base is a simple, flavorful, and creamy tomato sauce. The sauce incorporates a perfect blend of spices, tomato, cashew cream, chickpeas, and veggies. It's cozy comfort food—perfect for any season.

Prep Time: 15 minutes | Cook Time: 20 minutes | Yield: 4–6 servings

Ingredients

Sauce

¾ cup raw cashews

1 cup water

1 (15-ounce) can diced tomatoes

3 tablespoons tomato paste

1 tablespoon lime juice

2 teaspoons pure maple syrup (or other liquid sweetener) *or* 1–2 pitted dates, soaked

4 garlic cloves, peeled

1 tablespoon grated ginger or ginger paste

2 teaspoons garam masala

1 teaspoon smoked paprika

1 teaspoon chili powder

1 teaspoon ground cumin

1 teaspoon ground coriander

½ teaspoon ground turmeric

½ teaspoon sea salt or to taste

¼ teaspoon ground cinnamon

¼ teaspoon red pepper flakes

Tikka Masala

1 large onion, diced

1 red bell pepper, seeded and diced

1 green bell pepper, seeded and diced

1 (15-ounce) can chickpeas, drained and rinsed

1 (15-ounce) can diced tomatoes

Cooked brown rice, for serving

½ cup chopped fresh cilantro (optional)

½ cup unsweetened plant-based yogurt, store-bought (such as Kite Hill) or homemade (page 36) (optional)

1 lime, cut into wedges (optional)

Directions

1. Combine all the sauce ingredients in a high-powered blender and blend until smooth and creamy.

2. In a large pot, sauté the onion and bell peppers in a small amount of water over medium-high heat until tender. Add the chickpeas, tomatoes with their juices, and sauce mixture and turn the heat to high until the mixture begins to bubble. Reduce the heat to low, cover, and simmer for 15 minutes.

3. Serve the tikka masala over rice, topped with cilantro and yogurt and with lime wedges on the side for squeezing, if you like.

Chik'n Nuggets GF

Here's a fun way to use chickpeas that's convenient for lunch boxes, snacks, and appetizers. Each doughy ball of chickpeas is shaped and then smothered in bread crumbs. Kids and adults will love these with their favorite dipping sauce.

Prep Time: 20 minutes | Cook Time: 15–20 minutes | Yield: 4 servings

Ingredients

½ cup oat flour (gluten-free if necessary)

1 (15-ounce) can chickpeas, drained (liquid reserved) and rinsed

2 carrots, roughly chopped

1 teaspoon smoked paprika

1 teaspoon onion powder

½ teaspoon garlic powder

¼ teaspoon sea salt or to taste

2 teaspoons lemon juice

¼ cup unsweetened plant-based milk

¾ cup panko-style bread crumbs (gluten-free if necessary)

2 tablespoons nutritional yeast flakes

Barbecue sauce, ketchup, or hot sauce, for dipping

Tips & Hints

If you prefer a firmer and meatier consistency, try adding 2–3 tablespoons vital wheat gluten to the dough and increasing the aquafaba by 2–3 tablespoons.

Directions

1. Preheat the oven to 400°F. Line a rimmed baking sheet with parchment paper or a silicone mat.

2. Combine the flour, chickpeas, carrots, paprika, onion powder, garlic powder, and salt in a food processor and process until you have a dry, dough-like consistency. Transfer the dough to a large bowl.

3. Add the lemon juice and 3 tablespoons of the reserved chickpea liquid (aka aquafaba) to the dough and stir thoroughly to combine. You will begin to have a firm ball the consistency of thick cookie dough.

4. Portion the dough into 12 even pieces and form them into any shape you like.

5. Pour the milk into a small bowl. Combine the bread crumbs and nutritional yeast in another small bowl and mix well.

6. Dip each chickpea nugget into the milk and then coat thoroughly with the bread crumb mixture. Place the nuggets on the lined baking sheet and bake for 15–20 minutes or until golden. Serve with your favorite dipping sauce.

Coconut Curried Cauliflower and Butternut Squash /GF

This curry dish is a fragrant one-pot meal that features all the warm, sweet flavors of curry, squash, and coconut milk—it's perfect for those cool fall evenings. Butternut squash is plentiful in the fall, and you can find it already peeled and diced in most grocery stores.

Prep Time: 15 minutes | Cook Time: 30 minutes | Yield: 4 servings

Ingredients

1 red onion, diced

4–6 garlic cloves, minced

2 tablespoons grated ginger or ginger paste

2 tablespoons curry powder

1 cup low-sodium vegetable broth

2 tablespoons cornstarch

2½ cups 1-inch butternut squash cubes

1 small head cauliflower, cut into small florets

1 (13-ounce) can lite coconut milk

1 (15-ounce) can chickpeas, drained and rinsed

1 cup fresh or (thawed) frozen peas

2 teaspoons pure maple syrup (or other liquid sweetener)

½ teaspoon sea salt or to taste

Cooked brown rice or whole-grain pasta (gluten-free if necessary), for serving

Chopped fresh cilantro, for serving

Lime wedges, for serving

Directions

1. In a large skillet, sauté the onion in a small amount of water over medium-high heat until tender. Add the garlic, ginger, and curry powder and cook for 3–5 minutes.

2. In a small bowl, whisk together the broth and cornstarch until smooth. Add the broth mixture, butternut squash, cauliflower, coconut milk, chickpeas, peas, and maple syrup to the pot and mix well. Cover, turn down the heat to medium-low, and cook until the vegetables and squash are tender, 20–30 minutes. Season with salt and serve over rice or pasta, garnished with cilantro and lime wedges.

Tips & Hints

I like to add variety and color to this hearty winter stew by including our favorite veggies, such as chopped carrots, red bell peppers, or spinach.

Enchiladas with Mole Sauce

This recipe gets to the essence of a great enchilada, where the flavors build from the inside out. The luscious black bean filling is wrapped in corn tortillas and smothered with a simple yet decadent mole sauce, blending sweet and savory flavors. You'll never return to a red enchilada sauce again!

Prep Time: 30 minutes | Cook Time: 40 minutes | Yield: 4–6 servings

Ingredients

Mole Sauce

1 large onion, diced

4 garlic cloves

1 (15-ounce) can tomato sauce

1 cup water

3 tablespoons chili powder

3 tablespoons unsweetened cocoa powder

2 tablespoons all-natural peanut butter (100 percent peanuts) or almond butter

2 tablespoons pure maple syrup (or other liquid sweetener)

1½ tablespoons lime juice

1 teaspoon ancho chile powder

1 teaspoon ground cumin

½ teaspoon sea salt or to taste

½ teaspoon ground cinnamon

⅛ teaspoon ground allspice

Enchiladas

1 red onion, small diced

1 poblano pepper, small diced

1 red bell pepper, seeded and small diced

4 garlic cloves, minced

1 (15-ounce) can black beans, drained and rinsed

1 tablespoon lime juice

1 teaspoon ground cumin

½ teaspoon smoked paprika

½ teaspoon sea salt or to taste

2 cups chopped spinach or kale

10–12 (6-inch) corn tortillas

1 avocado, pitted, peeled, and diced

¼–½ cup chopped fresh cilantro

Directions

1. Preheat the oven to 350°F.

2. To make the mole sauce, in a large skillet, sauté the onion in a small amount of water over medium-high heat until translucent, slightly golden, and tender. Transfer the caramelized onion and remaining mole sauce ingredients to a blender and blend until smooth and creamy. Return the mole sauce to the same pan and simmer over low heat for 10–15 minutes.

3. Meanwhile, prepare the enchilada filling. In another large skillet, sauté the red onion, poblano pepper, bell pepper, and garlic in a small amount of water over medium-high heat until tender. Add the black beans, lime juice, cumin, smoked paprika, and salt and cook until heated through. Add the spinach or kale and cook just until wilted. Turn off the heat.

4. Wrap the tortillas in a slightly damp cloth or paper towel and microwave for 1–2 minutes or until softened.

5. Spoon a layer of the mole sauce in the bottom of a 9 × 13-inch baking pan. Place a tortilla on a work surface and brush or coat with a thin layer of mole sauce. Spoon about ¼ cup of the filling mixture on top and roll up tightly. Place the enchilada seam side down in the pan. Repeat with all the tortillas, placing the enchiladas side by side. If you have extra filling, simply add it between the rolled enchiladas and along the edges of the pan.

6. Pour the remaining mole sauce over the top of the enchiladas and bake for 10–15 minutes or until the sauce is hot and bubbly. (If you like, you can save a small amount of the mole sauce to spoon over your enchiladas when serving.)

7. Top the enchiladas with the diced avocado and cilantro and serve warm.

Chik'n Tamales with Tomatillo Sauce

Tamales are a popular Mexican street food consisting of stuffed masa shells wrapped in a corn husk. The stuffing used in this recipe is a combination of tangy and refreshing tomatillo sauce and hearty Soy Curls. Besides being delicious, this plant-based version uses no added oil or gluten. It doesn't get any better than an authentic Mexican tamale that's good for you too! There are many steps to tamale building, but it's not hard. And it's always fun to gather a few friends or family members to cook a delicious meal together.

Prep Time: 1 hour 15 minutes, plus 1 hour soaking time | Cook Time: 1 hour 15 minutes | Yield: 4–6 servings

Ingredients

Tamales and Filling

25 dried corn husks

4 ounces Butler Soy Curls

10 tomatillos, husked, rinsed, and halved

½ red onion, roughly chopped

2 jalapeño peppers, seeded if desired and chopped

1 cup chopped fresh cilantro

4 garlic cloves, peeled

2 tablespoons lime juice

2 teaspoons pure maple syrup (or other liquid sweetener) *or* 1 pitted date, soaked

½ teaspoon sea salt or to taste

¼ teaspoon black pepper

Dough

3 cups masa harina

2 teaspoons chili powder

1½ teaspoons baking powder

1 teaspoon ground cumin

1 teaspoon sea salt

1 cup mashed cooked sweet potatoes

2 cups warm low-sodium vegetable broth

Directions

Soak the Corn Husks

1. Place the corn husks in a large pot or bowl of very hot water, making sure to keep the husks submerged by placing a heavy bowl or plate on top of them. Let the husks soak for about 1 hour. (Alternatively, you can submerge them in boiling water, turn off the heat, and allow them to soak for 30 minutes.) Once the husks are soft and flexible, remove them from the water and wrap them in a damp towel until ready to use.

Make the Filling

2. While the corn husks are soaking, put the Soy Curls in a medium-size bowl and cover with warm water. Soak for 10 minutes or until fully rehydrated. Drain, then pulse in a food processor until crumbly but not mushy. Transfer to a medium-size bowl.

3. Turn on the oven broiler. Line a rimmed baking sheet with parchment paper or a silicone mat.

4. Put the tomatillos and onion on the lined baking sheet and broil until charred and softened, 8–10 minutes.

5. Transfer the roasted tomatillos and onion to a blender. Add the jalapeños, cilantro, garlic, lime juice, maple syrup or date, salt, and pepper and process until well combined—you can fully puree the mixture or leave it a bit chunky if you prefer. Set aside about half of the tomatillo mixture for topping the tamales. Add the other half of the tomatillo sauce to the bowl of Soy Curls and mix to coat. Set aside.

Make the Dough

6. In a large bowl, whisk together the masa harina, chili powder, baking powder, cumin, and salt. Add the mashed sweet potatoes and about half of the warm broth and begin to combine the ingredients with your hands. Continue adding the broth little by little until a very soft dough begins to form. The dough should be the consistency of very soft play dough or creamy peanut butter. Add more broth, 1 tablespoon at a time, if the texture is not soft enough.

7. Cover the dough to keep it from drying out. If it becomes too dry, add more broth as needed.

Assemble the Tamales

8. Place a corn husk, smooth side up, on a work surface, with the wide end closest to you and the tapered end pointing away from you. Using your hands or a silicone spatula, spread about ¼ cup of the dough in a large rectangle on the husk. Leave ½–1 inch of space at the wide end so the dough doesn't burst out once it begins cooking, and leave 2–3 inches of space at the tapered end so you have room to fold the husk.

9. Spoon 2 tablespoons of the filling lengthwise down the center of the dough. Fold in one long side of the husk over the filling. Fold in the other long side so that it overlaps the first (it's like folding a trifold brochure), and gently pinch the masa together. Fold the bottom end over and set aside the tamale with the folded side down. (If you like, you can secure each tamale by tying a thin strip of corn husk around it.) Repeat to assemble the remaining tamales.

Steam the Tamales

10. Pour 1–2 inches of water into a large pot and set a steamer basket inside. Make sure the water comes up to just below the basket.

11. Place 2 or 3 corn husks in the steamer basket and place the tamales on top, positioning them upright with their open end up.

12. Lay a wet towel or a few corn husks over the top of the tamales. Cover the pot and bring the water to a boil. Reduce the heat to a simmer and steam for 45–60 minutes. To test for doneness, remove one tamale and try to pull the husk off. If the husk pulls away easily from the tamale, it's done. If the dough is still sticky or wet, cook the tamales for 5–10 more minutes and recheck.

13. Allow the tamales to cool for 10 minutes, then serve topped with the reserved tomatillo sauce.

Tips & Hints

To cook the tamales in an Instant Pot, set it to "manual" and "high pressure" for 25 minutes. Allow the pressure to naturally release for 10 minutes, then quick release.

Seaside Lime Tacos

The ever-popular California fish taco has not been forgotten in my kitchen. The special components in this recipe are the artichokes and creamy lime dressing. We love these easy, fun plant-based tacos.

Prep Time: 20 minutes | Cook Time: 15 minutes | Yield: 4 servings

Ingredients

1 cup whole-wheat flour (or oat flour for gluten-free)

1 cup unsweetened plant-based milk

2 cups panko-style bread crumbs (gluten-free if necessary)

¼ cup nutritional yeast flakes

2 teaspoons Old Bay Seasoning

1 teaspoon garlic powder

1 nori sheet, toasted and crumbled

2 (14-ounce) cans artichokes, drained, rinsed, and quartered

Lime Dressing

1 large ripe avocado, pitted and peeled

2 garlic cloves, peeled

1 jalapeño pepper, seeded

½ cup cilantro leaves

½ cup water

2 tablespoons lime juice

2 tablespoons apple cider vinegar

1½ tablespoons pure maple syrup (or other liquid sweetener)

¼ teaspoon ground cumin

¼ teaspoon sea salt or to taste

For Serving

1 (8-ounce) package shredded cabbage or coleslaw mix

8 (6-ounce) corn tortillas

1–2 tablespoons sriracha

2 limes, sliced

¼ cup chopped fresh cilantro

Directions

1. Preheat the oven to 400°F. Line a rimmed baking sheet with parchment paper or a silicone mat.

2. Line up three shallow bowls. In the first bowl, put the flour. In the second bowl, put the milk. In the third bowl, combine the bread crumbs, nutritional yeast, Old Bay, garlic powder, and crumbled nori.

3. One at a time, dip the artichoke quarters in the flour, covering completely; then in the milk; and then in the panko mixture, coating well. Place on the lined baking sheet. Bake for 10–15 minutes or until the breading is golden brown.

4. Meanwhile, combine all the dressing ingredients in a blender and blend until smooth and creamy.

5. Put the cabbage or coleslaw in a bowl, add half of the dressing, and toss until thoroughly combined. Reserve the remaining dressing to drizzle over the tacos.

6. Put 4 tortillas on a plate, cover with a damp paper towel, and microwave on high for 30–60 seconds or until they are warm and pliable. Repeat with the remaining 4 tortillas.

7. To assemble the tacos, put several artichokes on each warm tortilla and top with slaw and lime dressing. Garnish with sriracha, limes, and cilantro.

Tips & Hints

Breaded artichokes are a delicious appetizer all alone with almost any type of dipping sauce. If you like them more or less "fishy" flavored, simply add more nori or omit it depending on personal preference.

Toasting nori sheets makes them crisp and easy to crumble. Place nori sheets on a baking sheet and bake at 200°F for about 2 minutes or until crispy.

Indian Vegetable Korma

This delicious Indian dish is loaded with a colorful vegetable medley and smothered in a fragrant cream sauce. The best part of this recipe is that you can add whatever vegetable mix you like. The sauce is the star of the show and will make any veggie combination burst with flavor! Serve over warm rice, quinoa, or naan bread.

Prep Time: 15 minutes | Cook Time: 25 minutes | Yield: 4–6 servings

Ingredients

Korma

- 1 red bell pepper, seeded and large diced
- 1 green bell pepper, seeded and large diced
- 1 small red onion, diced
- 2 carrots, diced
- ½ head cauliflower, chopped
- 1 sweet potato, peeled and cubed
- 1 cup fresh or (thawed) frozen peas
- 1 cup water

Sauce

- 2 cups unsweetened plant-based milk
- ¼ cup canned lite coconut milk
- 3 tablespoons tomato paste
- 4 teaspoons cornstarch
- 1 tablespoon curry powder
- 1 tablespoon grated ginger or ginger paste
- 2 teaspoons pure maple syrup (or other liquid sweetener)
- 1 teaspoon garam masala

- 1 teaspoon garlic powder *or* 4–5 garlic cloves, minced
- 1 teaspoon onion powder
- 1 teaspoon fennel seeds
- ¾ teaspoon ground cumin
- ¼ teaspoon red pepper flakes
- ¾–1 teaspoon sea salt or to taste
- ¼ teaspoon black pepper

Directions

1. Combine the bell peppers, onion, carrots, cauliflower, sweet potato, peas, and water in a large pot. Cover and simmer over medium heat until the vegetables are tender and the potato softens, 12–14 minutes. If the water evaporates and the vegetables dry out, add a little more water.

2. While the veggies are cooking, combine all the sauce ingredients in a blender and blend until smooth and creamy.

3. Add the sauce to the pot of vegetables and cook until the sauce is bubbly and thickened. Turn the heat down to low and cook for another 10–15 minutes.

Tips & Hints

This recipe is easy to customize with any vegetable combination or even chickpeas. Feel free to throw everything into a slow cooker and walk away, allowing the korma to simmer for 4–5 hours on low.

Jackfruit Crabless Cakes

In my youth, I was a huge fan of shellfish and loved all things seafood. This medley of green jackfruit, Old Bay Seasoning, nori seaweed, and mayo comes together to re-create traditional crab cakes. The texture is fantastic and the flavor profile is spot on.

Prep Time: 25 minutes | Cook Time: 15–18 minutes | Yield: 10–12 cakes

Ingredients

Horseradish Dill Aioli

1 cup vegan mayonnaise, store-bought or homemade (page 131)

3 tablespoons prepared horseradish

1 tablespoon dried dill

2 teaspoons lemon juice

¼ teaspoon sea salt or to taste

⅛ teaspoon black pepper to taste

Crabless Cakes

1 (20-ounce) can young green jackfruit in water, drained

1 (15-ounce) can chickpeas, drained (liquid reserved) and rinsed

½ cup oat flour

3–4 green onions, thinly sliced

½ cup finely chopped celery

¼ cup chopped fresh cilantro or flat-leaf parsley

¼ cup vegan mayonnaise, store-bought or homemade (page 131)

1 nori sheet, toasted and crumbled

1–2 tablespoons Old Bay Seasoning

1 tablespoon lemon juice

1 teaspoon ground mustard

1 teaspoon vegan Worcestershire sauce

½ teaspoon black pepper

1 cup panko-style bread crumbs (gluten-free if necessary)

Directions

1. Preheat the oven to 400°F. Line a rimmed baking sheet with parchment paper or a silicone mat.

2. In a small bowl, whisk together all the aioli ingredients. Cover and refrigerate until ready to serve.

3. Put the jackfruit in a food processor and pulse 6–8 times, just until the pieces are broken up, resembling crabmeat. Transfer the jackfruit to a large bowl.

4. Put the chickpeas and ¼ cup of the reserved chickpea liquid (aka aquafaba) in the food processor and pulse until finely chopped and lumpy (do not process into a paste).

5. Add the chickpea mixture to the bowl with the jackfruit. Add the flour, green onions, celery, cilantro or parsley, mayonnaise, nori, Old Bay, lemon juice, mustard, Worcestershire sauce, and pepper and mix well. Form the mixture into 10–12 patties.

6. Put the panko in a shallow bowl. Lightly press each patty into the panko until thoroughly coated. Place the patties on the lined baking sheet and bake for 15–18 minutes or until golden brown. Serve immediately with the aioli.

Tips & Hints

Instead of horseradish, feel free to add your choice of herbs to the aioli.

Toasting nori sheets makes them crisp and easy to crumble. Place nori sheets on a baking sheet and bake at 200°F for about 2 minutes or until crispy.

Mediterranean Green Falafel

Green falafel is a classic Middle Eastern and Mediterranean dish, and one of the most popular fast foods served on the streets of Syria, Israel, and Egypt. It takes the form of delicious little veggie balls loaded with chickpeas, herbs, and lots of spices and is traditionally served inside a warm pita and topped with cucumbers, tomatoes, and lemon tahini sauce. You can also serve falafel on top of a fresh green salad.

Prep Time: 15 minutes, plus 8 hours soaking time | Cook Time: 25–30 minutes | Yield: 4 servings (22–24 falafel)

Ingredients

Falafel

1 cup dried chickpeas

½ medium red onion

1 cup fresh flat-leaf parsley leaves

1 cup fresh cilantro leaves

¼ cup fresh mint leaves

1 jalapeño pepper, seeded and ribs removed

3 garlic cloves, peeled

Grated zest of 1 lemon

2 tablespoons lemon juice

1 teaspoon baking powder

1 teaspoon ground coriander

½ teaspoon ground cumin

¼ teaspoon ground cardamom

½ teaspoon sea salt or to taste

½ teaspoon red pepper flakes

For Serving

4–6 whole-wheat or gluten-free pita pockets, warmed

1 cup diced cucumber

1 cup diced tomato

½ medium red onion, thinly sliced

Lemon Tahini Dressing (page 133)

Directions

1. Rinse the chickpeas, put them in a medium bowl, and cover with plenty of water (the chickpeas will triple in size!). Put the bowl in the refrigerator and allow the chickpeas to soak for 8–10 hours.

2. Preheat the oven to 400°F. Line a rimmed baking sheet with parchment paper or a silicone mat.

3. Drain and rinse the chickpeas and put them in a food processor. Add the remaining falafel ingredients and process until the mixture reaches a fine grainy texture.

4. Scoop out about 2 tablespoons of the dough mixture and form it into a small ball or patty. Place it on the lined baking sheet and repeat with the rest of the mixture. Bake the falafel for 25–30 minutes, flipping halfway through, or until golden brown around the edges and dry to the touch.

5. Serve the falafel inside the warm pita, topped with cucumber, tomato, red onion, and lemon tahini dressing.

Tips & Hints

Use only dried and soaked chickpeas for this recipe. Canned chickpeas are too soft and wet.

Warm pita bread by wrapping them in aluminum foil and placing them in the oven for 10 minutes at 350°F. Alternately, place a damp paper towel on a plate, place pita bread on the paper towel, and microwave for 30–45 seconds.

Baked falafel freezes beautifully!

One-Pot Mushroom Stroganoff

This creamy mushroom dish is loaded with the flavors of traditional stroganoff. One pot is all you need to cook this meal, making cleanup easy. Any kind of mushrooms work well in this recipe, so experiment with different types to find out what you like best. Wild mushrooms are our favorite.

Prep Time: 20 minutes | Cook Time: 20 minutes | Yield: 6 servings

Ingredients

1 onion, diced

¼ cup dry white wine (optional)

4–6 garlic cloves, minced

2 cups low-sodium vegetable broth

2 cups unsweetened plant-based milk

2 tablespoons Dijon mustard

2 tablespoons cornstarch

2 tablespoons nutritional yeast flakes

1 tablespoon low-sodium tamari or soy sauce

1 tablespoon vegan Worcestershire sauce

1 tablespoon paprika

1 teaspoon onion powder

½ teaspoon sea salt or to taste

¼ teaspoon black pepper

1 pound mushrooms (any type), sliced

1 (6-ounce) can pitted black olives, drained and sliced

12 ounces whole-grain rotini or other pasta (gluten-free if necessary)

5 ounces spinach

¼ teaspoon red pepper flakes

Directions

1. In a large pot, sauté the onion in the wine or a small amount of water over high heat until translucent. Add the garlic and turn off the heat.

2. Add the broth, milk, mustard, cornstarch, nutritional yeast, tamari or soy sauce, Worcestershire sauce, paprika, onion powder, salt, and pepper and whisk until thoroughly combined.

3. Add the mushrooms, olives, and pasta and bring to a boil, then reduce to a simmer and cover the pot. Cook for 15 minutes or until the pasta is al dente, stirring occasionally to prevent sticking.

4. Add the spinach and stir until fully wilted and incorporated into the pasta. Top with the red pepper flakes and serve.

Tips & Hints

Try adding extra veggies, such as peas, sun-dried tomatoes, and roasted red peppers.

Build a Poke Bowl

Hawaiian poke bowls combine a medley of flavors and textures. The ingredients are similar to those of a sushi roll, except that you can choose the amount of rice, veggies, and sauce you add to your bowl. So line up your own poke bowl bar and let everyone customize their meal to their preference!

Prep Time: 30 minutes | Yield: 4–6 servings

Ingredients

Sweet Rice

3–4 cups cooked short-grain brown rice or black rice

2 nori sheets, toasted and crumbled

¼ cup rice vinegar

1 tablespoon pure maple syrup (or other liquid sweetener)

1 tablespoon low-sodium tamari or soy sauce

Sriracha Aioli

½ cup vegan mayonnaise, store-bought or homemade (page 131)

1–2 tablespoons sriracha

Ponzu Sauce

½ cup orange juice

¼ cup low-sodium tamari

¼ cup water

2 tablespoons lime juice

1 tablespoon rice vinegar

1 teaspoon sriracha

Toppings

2 cups mixed greens

½ cup shredded red cabbage

2 carrots, shredded

1 cucumber, diced

2 cups (thawed) frozen edamame or baked tofu

1 avocado, pitted, peeled, and cubed

1 mango, pitted, peeled, and cubed

4 green onions, thinly sliced

Sesame seeds

Pickled ginger

Chopped fresh cilantro

1 lime, cut into wedges

Directions

1. To make the sweet rice, in a medium bowl, toss the cooked rice with the nori, vinegar, maple syrup, and tamari or soy sauce. Set aside.

2. To make the sriracha aioli, in a small bowl (or in a small squirt bottle), stir together the mayonnaise and sriracha. Set aside.

3. To make the ponzu sauce, in another small bowl (or in another small squirt bottle), whisk together all the ponzu sauce ingredients. Set aside.

4. To serve, put all the topping items in individual bowls. For each poke bowl, scoop a hearty serving of rice into a bowl. Invite people to choose the toppings they enjoy and to finish with plenty of sriracha aioli and ponzu sauce.

Tips & Hints

For the aioli, you can use 2 teaspoons wasabi powder instead of the sriracha for a fun variation.

Toasting nori sheets makes them crisp and easy to crumble. Place nori sheets on a baking sheet and bake at 200°F for about 2 minutes or until crispy.

Bell Pepper Quiche

This oil-free quiche uses bell peppers for the crust, which makes preparation so simple. The filling is a creamy tofu-based "cheese" loaded with plenty of hearty potatoes, spinach, and asparagus. You can prep everything ahead of time and bake the quiche when you're ready. The vegan hollandaise sauce drizzled over the top adds some extra zing.

Prep time: 25 minutes | Cook Time: 30 minutes | Yield: 4 servings

Ingredients

- 1 (14-ounce) package extra-firm tofu, drained
- ⅓ cup nutritional yeast flakes
- 2 tablespoons tahini
- 1 tablespoon chopped fresh thyme *or* 1 teaspoon dried thyme
- 1 tablespoon chopped fresh rosemary *or* 1 teaspoon dried rosemary
- 2 teaspoons onion powder
- 1 teaspoon garlic powder
- ½ teaspoon sea salt or to taste
- ¼ teaspoon black pepper
- 2 cups frozen oil-free shredded hash brown potatoes (such as Trader Joe's or Cascadian Farm)
- 2 cups chopped fresh or (thawed and well-drained) frozen spinach
- 10 asparagus stalks, cut into ½-inch pieces (optional)
- 3 medium bell peppers (red, orange, and/or yellow), halved and seeded
- Hollandaise Sauce (page 132), for serving

Directions

1. Preheat the oven to 375°F. Line a 9 × 13-inch baking pan with parchment paper.

2. In a food processor, combine the tofu, nutritional yeast, tahini, thyme, rosemary, onion powder, garlic powder, salt, and pepper. Process until the mixture has the consistency of ricotta cheese.

3. Transfer the tofu mixture to a large bowl. Fold in the potatoes, spinach, and asparagus (if using) and mix until well incorporated.

4. Place the bell pepper halves in the lined baking pan, cut side up. Generously fill each bell pepper half with the tofu filling.

5. Bake for 30 minutes or until the tops are golden brown. Remove from the oven and allow to sit for 15 minutes. Drizzle each quiche with 1–2 tablespoons of hollandaise sauce and serve.

Tips & Hints

Instead of using frozen potatoes, you can bake or boil 2 medium potatoes and allow them to chill in the refrigerator for a few hours. Then shred the cooled potatoes and add them to the recipe. Do not use raw shredded potato in this recipe.

Samosa Burritos GF

Baked samosas are a healthy version of a traditional fried pastry. Potatoes and cauliflower are combined with the perfect blend of Indian spices, wrapped in a tortilla, then baked and served with a mint and cilantro chutney. These samosa burritos burst with flavor—a flavor loved by kids and adults alike.

Prep Time: 20 minutes | Cook Time: 35 minutes | Yield: 4–6 servings

Ingredients

- 2 cups roughly chopped cauliflower
- 2 cups medium-diced potatoes
- 1 red onion, small diced
- 1 jalapeño pepper, seeded and finely diced
- 4–5 garlic cloves, minced
- 2 teaspoons grated ginger or ginger paste
- 1 teaspoon garam masala
- ½ teaspoon ground cumin
- ½ teaspoon ground coriander
- ½ teaspoon fennel seeds, toasted
- ¼ teaspoon ground turmeric
- 1 cup fresh or frozen peas
- 1 tablespoon lemon juice
- ¾ teaspoon sea salt or to taste
- ½ teaspoon black pepper
- 8 large whole-grain or gluten-free tortillas
- Mint Yogurt Chutney (page 132), for serving

Directions

1. Preheat the oven to 400°F. Line a rimmed baking sheet with parchment paper or a silicone mat.

2. Bring a large pot of water to a boil. Add the cauliflower and potatoes and cook over medium-high heat until tender. Drain and set aside.

3. In a large skillet, sauté the onion and jalapeño in a small amount of water over medium-high heat until tender. Add the garlic, ginger, garam masala, cumin, coriander, fennel seeds, and turmeric. Turn the heat down to medium and sauté for 5 minutes more.

4. Add the cauliflower and potatoes, peas, and lemon juice and thoroughly combine, lightly smashing the potatoes and cauliflower. Season with the salt and pepper and cook for 10 minutes.

5. Put 4 tortillas on a plate, cover with a damp paper towel, and microwave on high for 30–60 seconds or until they are warm and pliable. Repeat with the remaining 4 tortillas.

6. Scoop ½–¾ cup of the potato mixture onto each warm tortilla. Be careful not to overfill, which can make the tortillas difficult to roll. Fold the sides

of the tortilla over the potato mixture and gently roll up like a burrito. (Or, if you like, you can make triangles for a classic samosa look.) Place the burritos seam side down on the lined baking sheet and bake for 10–15 minutes or until golden brown and crispy. Serve warm, topped with the chutney.

Tips & Hints

If you're looking for a shortcut, you can use frozen oil-free hash browns and frozen cauliflower florets to reduce some of the prep time.

Toast the fennel seeds by placing the seeds in a dry skillet over medium heat and stirring continuously for about 2–3 minutes, until golden and fragrant.

Scalloped Veggies au Gratin

When I was growing up, my mother made traditional scalloped potatoes, which was one of the meals I requested most. So I took her much-loved classic casserole and added a few of my favorite veggies, and reinvented her white sauce into a vegan cheese sauce. Layers of potatoes, zucchini, carrots, and mushrooms, plus a creamy Alfredo-style sauce, all make this dish finger-licking good. No oil, no dairy, no meat . . . just pure plant-based goodness going on here!

Prep Time: 20 minutes | Cook Time: 1 hour 20 minutes | Yield: 4–6 servings

Ingredients

Sauce

3 cups unsweetened plant-based milk

1 cup raw cashews or hemp seeds

¼ cup nutritional yeast flakes

1½ tablespoons cornstarch

1 tablespoon miso paste

2 teaspoons lemon juice

2 teaspoons Dijon mustard

1 teaspoon onion powder

½ teaspoon garlic powder

½ teaspoon sea salt or to taste

½ teaspoon black pepper

⅛ teaspoon ground nutmeg

Veggies

2 pounds Yukon Gold potatoes (about 4–6 medium)

1 large onion, thinly sliced

8–10 ounces mushrooms (any type), sliced

5–6 garlic cloves, minced

2 teaspoons chopped fresh thyme *or* ¾ teaspoon dried thyme

2 teaspoons chopped fresh sage *or* ¾ teaspoon dried sage

1 zucchini, thinly sliced

3 carrots, shredded

1 cup whole-grain bread crumbs (gluten-free if necessary)

½ teaspoon smoked paprika (optional)

Directions

1. Preheat the oven to 375°F. Line a 9 × 13-inch baking pan with parchment paper.

2. Combine all the sauce ingredients in a high-powered blender and puree until smooth. Set aside.

3. Peel and thinly slice the potatoes, then put the slices in a bowl and cover with cool water to prevent browning. Set aside.

4. In a nonstick skillet, sauté the onion and mushrooms in a small amount of water over medium-high heat until tender, 4–5 minutes. Add the garlic, thyme, and sage during the last minute of cooking.

5. Drain the potatoes. Arrange half of the potato slices, half of the zucchini and carrots, and half of the sautéed mushrooms and onion in an overlapping layer in the lined baking pan. Pour half of the sauce over the vegetables. Repeat with the remaining vegetables and sauce. Top with the bread crumbs and smoked paprika (if using).

6. Cover the pan with aluminum foil and bake for 50–60 minutes or until the potatoes are fork-tender and soft. Uncover and bake for 15 more minutes or until the top is golden and bubbly. Serve warm.

Tips & Hints

A mandoline slicer will allow you to get perfectly uniform potato slices and save time in the kitchen. Watch your fingers!

You can parboil the potato slices for 10–12 minutes before assembly to reduce the baking time.

Smoky Mushroom Boscaiola

Boscaiola is a creamy, rustic mushroom sauce loaded with the earthy flavors of mushrooms and garlic. Smoked paprika adds that perfect hint of smokiness for comfort food at its best.

Prep Time: 20 minutes | Cook Time: 15 minutes | Yield: 4 servings

Ingredients

1 onion, cut in half and thinly sliced

¼ cup dry white wine

1 pound mushrooms (any type), sliced

¾ cup raw cashews

1 cup water

1 cup unsweetened plant-based milk

5 garlic cloves, peeled

2 tablespoons Dijon mustard

2 tablespoons nutritional yeast flakes

1 tablespoon vegan Worcestershire sauce

1 tablespoon smoked paprika

½ teaspoon sea salt or to taste

¼ teaspoon black pepper

4 cups cooked whole-grain rice, pasta, or gnocchi, for serving

Directions

1. In a large skillet, sauté the onion in the wine over medium-high heat until slightly browned. Add the mushrooms and cook for 5–7 minutes or until the mushrooms are tender.

2. In a high-powered blender, combine the cashews, water, milk, garlic, mustard, nutritional yeast, Worcestershire sauce, smoked paprika, salt, and pepper and blend until smooth and creamy.

3. Add the cream sauce to the skillet and cook over medium heat until bubbly and thickened. Serve right away over rice, pasta, or gnocchi.

Spanish Vegetable Paella

Paella is a traditional Spanish dish that brings rice, vegetables, and mouthwatering flavors to the table. It's a simple family-style meal that's served right from the pot. When our daughter traveled to Spain and came home raving about paella, I decided to create a whole food, plant-based, oil-free version that we all could enjoy. The flavors begin with beautiful saffron-infused rice and an assortment of herbs and spices that are sure to warm your belly.

Prep Time: 30 minutes | Cook Time: 1 hour 15 minutes | Yield: 6 servings

Ingredients

- 3 cups low-sodium vegetable broth
- 1½ cups short-grain brown rice
- Pinch of saffron threads *or* 1 teaspoon ground turmeric
- 1 red onion, medium diced
- 5 garlic cloves, chopped
- 1 red bell pepper, seeded and sliced
- 2 carrots, shredded
- 8–10 ounces mushrooms (any type), sliced

- 1 cup green beans, cut into 2-inch pieces
- 2 teaspoons chopped fresh rosemary *or* ½ teaspoon dried rosemary
- 1 teaspoon chopped fresh thyme *or* ½ teaspoon dried thyme
- 1 teaspoon smoked paprika
- 1 teaspoon sea salt or to taste
- ½ teaspoon black pepper
- ½ teaspoon red pepper flakes
- 1 (15-ounce) can diced fire-roasted tomatoes

- ¼ cup dry red wine
- 1 tablespoon vegan Worcestershire sauce
- 1 tablespoon low-sodium tamari or soy sauce
- 1 cup (thawed) frozen peas
- ½ cup sliced kalamata olives
- 1 (14-ounce) can artichokes, drained and rinsed
- 1 lemon, cut into wedges
- ¼ cup chopped fresh flat-leaf parsley (optional)

Directions

1. In a medium saucepan, combine the broth, rice, and saffron threads or turmeric and bring to a boil. Reduce the heat to low, cover, and allow the rice to simmer for 45 minutes or until tender.

2. In a large skillet, sauté the onion in a small amount of water over medium-high heat until tender. Add the garlic, bell pepper, carrots, mushrooms, green beans, rosemary, thyme, smoked paprika, salt, black pepper, and red pepper flakes and continue to cook for 10–12 minutes or until the vegetables are tender.

3. Add the tomatoes with their juices, wine, Worcestershire sauce, and tamari or soy sauce. Turn the heat down to medium and cook for 10–12 minutes.

4. Add the cooked brown rice to the skillet, turn the heat down to low, and cook for 10 minutes. Turn off the heat.

5. Top the paella with the peas, olives, and artichokes and allow the pan to sit for 10 minutes. Serve warm, topped with lemon wedges and parsley (if using).

Tips & Hints

To speed things up, feel free to cook the rice in an Instant Pot. Use only 2 cups vegetable broth and cook on high pressure for 20 minutes with a quick release.

For a true one-pot paella, use parboiled rice so you can cook it directly in the pot with the rest of the ingredients. Simply add 1½ cups parboiled brown rice, the saffron or turmeric, and 3 cups vegetable broth to the pan along with the other ingredients in step 3.

Spinach Artichoke Pasta Bake

Adapting traditional recipes is a creative challenge that I love tackling. During our ten-day Jumpstart programs at PlantPure, we have used many classic family recipes to introduce people to the plant-based lifestyle and show them that going plant-based doesn't mean sacrificing flavor. This recipe originally came from a Betty Crocker magazine, but I made it plant-based with just a few simple tweaks. A heavy spinach artichoke dip turned into a hearty, delicious casserole with an assortment of colorful veggies—and with less than half of the fat calories!

Prep Time: 15 minutes | Cook Time: 35 minutes | Yield: 6 servings

Ingredients

"Cheese" Sauce

¾ cup raw cashews

1 cup water

1 cup unsweetened plant-based milk

2 teaspoons lemon juice

4 garlic cloves, peeled

3 tablespoons nutritional yeast flakes

2 teaspoons Dijon mustard

½ teaspoon sea salt or salt to taste

½ teaspoon black pepper

⅛ teaspoon ground nutmeg

Pasta Bake

10 ounces whole-grain rotini pasta (gluten-free if necessary)

8 ounces Butler Soy Curls

1 red onion, diced

1 red bell pepper, seeded and diced

6 garlic cloves, minced

½ teaspoon red pepper flakes

1 (14-ounce) can artichoke hearts, drained and coarsely chopped

1 (12–14-ounce) package frozen chopped spinach, thawed

Sea salt and black pepper to taste

1 cup whole-grain bread crumbs (gluten-free if necessary)

3 tablespoons nutritional yeast flakes

Directions

1. Preheat the oven to 375°F. Line a 9 × 13-inch baking pan with parchment paper.

2. Combine all the "cheese" sauce ingredients in a high-powered blender and blend until smooth and creamy. Set aside.

3. Cook the pasta according to the package instructions. Drain.

4. Meanwhile, put the Soy Curls in a bowl and cover with warm water. Soak for 10 minutes or until fully rehydrated. Drain.

5. In a large skillet, sauté the onion, bell pepper, garlic, and red pepper flakes in a small amount of water over medium heat until the onion is tender.

6. In a large bowl, combine the cooked pasta, rehydrated Soy Curls, sautéed onion mixture, artichokes, spinach, and "cheese" sauce. Mix until thoroughly combined, then season with salt and pepper.

7. Transfer the mixture to the lined baking pan. Top with the bread crumbs and nutritional yeast. Bake for 20–30 minutes or until golden. Serve warm.

Tips & Hints

You can add other veggies, such as peas or carrots, if you are looking for a bigger or different variety of veggies.

Sweet-and-Sour Soy Curls

If you're missing the traditional flavors of sweet-and-sour chicken, this recipe hits the mark. The sauce has no added sugars, just sweet pineapple for the perfect flavor balance. This dish is quick, easy, and fun to serve to any crowd.

Prep Time: 20 minutes | **Cook Time: 15 minutes** | **Yield: 4 servings**

Ingredients

4 ounces Butler Soy Curls

1 cup drained canned crushed pineapple (in its own juice with no added syrups)

1 tablespoon grated ginger or ginger paste

4 garlic cloves, peeled

½ cup water

3 tablespoons red wine vinegar

1 tablespoon cornstarch

1½ teaspoons sriracha

½ teaspoon sea salt or to taste

¼ teaspoon black pepper

1 onion, sliced

1 red bell pepper, seeded and sliced

1 yellow bell pepper, seeded and sliced

4 celery stalks, sliced

4–6 green onions, sliced

4 cups cooked brown rice, quinoa, or pasta, for serving

¼ cup sesame seeds

Directions

1. Put the Soy Curls in a bowl and cover with warm water. Soak for 10 minutes or until fully rehydrated. Drain.

2. Combine the pineapple, ginger, garlic, water, vinegar, cornstarch, sriracha, salt, and black pepper in a blender and blend until smooth and creamy. Set aside.

3. In a large skillet, sauté the onion in a small amount of water over medium-high heat until it begins to brown around the edges. Add the rehydrated Soy Curls, bell peppers, celery, green onions, and pineapple sauce and cook for 4–6 minutes or until the veggies are slightly tender and the sauce becomes bubbly and thick.

4. Serve warm over rice, quinoa, or pasta, topped with the sesame seeds.

Thai Tacos GF

This recipe takes Taco Tuesday to another level. Mexican and Thai come together for a fun and flavor-packed fusion taco. Combining different world cuisines on the same plate is a great way to experiment with spices, flavors, and unfamiliar ingredients. Here, the vibrant flavors, including an array of spices, are infused into the meaty cauliflower and walnut taco filling. The whole taco is topped with a sweet-and-sour cabbage and mango or pineapple coleslaw and a savory peanut sauce.

Prep Time: 30 minutes | Cook Time: 45 minutes | Yield: 10–12 tacos

Ingredients

Sweet-and-Sour Slaw

- 1 (14-ounce) bag shredded cabbage or coleslaw mix
- 2 cups finely chopped fresh or (thawed) frozen mango or pineapple
- 4 green onions, thinly sliced
- ¼ cup chopped fresh cilantro
- 2 tablespoons rice vinegar
- 1 tablespoon lime juice
- ¼ teaspoon sea salt or to taste

Tacos

- 10–12 (6-inch) corn tortillas
- 1 (12-ounce) head cauliflower *or* 1 (1-pound) bag (thawed) frozen riced cauliflower
- 1½ cups walnuts
- 2 tablespoons lime juice
- 2 tablespoons low-sodium tamari or soy sauce
- 1½ teaspoons pure maple syrup (or other liquid sweetener)
- 1 teaspoon grated ginger or ginger paste
- 1 teaspoon sriracha
- 1 teaspoon garlic powder
- 1 teaspoon onion powder
- 1 teaspoon ground coriander
- 1 teaspoon chili powder

Peanut Sauce

- 3 tablespoons all-natural peanut butter (100 percent peanuts)
- 2 garlic cloves, peeled
- 2 tablespoons water
- 2 tablespoons lime juice
- 1 tablespoon rice vinegar
- 1 tablespoon low-sodium tamari or soy sauce
- 1 teaspoon grated ginger or ginger paste
- 1 teaspoon sriracha

Garnish (optional)

- ½ cup crushed peanuts
- ½ cup chopped fresh cilantro

Directions

1. Preheat the oven to 375°F. Line a rimmed baking sheet with parchment paper or a silicone mat.

2. Combine all the slaw ingredients in a medium bowl and toss. Cover and refrigerate until ready to serve.

3. Wrap the tortillas in a slightly damp cloth or paper towel and microwave for 30 seconds. Drape each tortilla over two bars of an oven rack and bake for 8–10 minutes to crisp up into a taco shell shape. Watch the tortillas carefully as they can burn quickly. Remove and set aside.

4. Combine the cauliflower and walnuts in a food processor and pulse until evenly ground into rice-size pieces. Transfer the mixture to a large bowl and add the lime juice, tamari or soy sauce, maple syrup, ginger, sriracha, garlic powder, onion powder, coriander, and chili powder. Mix thoroughly until well combined.

5. Evenly spread the cauliflower-walnut filling on the lined baking sheet and bake for 30–40 minutes, stirring midway through to prevent burning around the edges.

6. While the filling is baking, combine all the peanut sauce ingredients in a blender and blend until smooth and creamy.

7. To build the tacos, spoon the cauliflower-walnut filling into the taco shells, then add the mango or pineapple slaw. Top with the peanut sauce and your choice of garnish.

Tips & Hints

You can skip the taco shells and serve the filling and slaw in a lettuce bowl or on top of a bed of greens. The filling and slaw pair beautifully with a baked sweet potato.

For those of you who love a meatier texture, you can replace the cauliflower-walnut filling with Butler Soy Curls.

Thai Green Curried Potatoes

This vegetable dish is loaded with the unique flavors of traditional Thai curry. It's chock-full of potatoes and mixed vegetables covered with a creamy, flavorful curry sauce. Feel free to change up the veggies to your taste preferences. This recipe is all about the sauce!

Prep Time: 15 minutes | **Cook Time: 30 minutes** | **Yield: 4 servings**

Ingredients

- 1 pound red potatoes (about 3 medium potatoes), cut into 2-inch chunks
- 8 ounces green beans, cut into 2-inch pieces
- 1 cup canned lite coconut milk
- ½ cup unsweetened plant-based milk
- ¼ cup Thai green curry paste (such as Thai Kitchen)
- 1 tablespoon cornstarch
- 1 tablespoon pure maple syrup (or other liquid sweetener)
- 2 teaspoons lime juice
- ½ teaspoon sea salt or to taste
- ¼ teaspoon red pepper flakes (optional)
- 1 onion, diced
- 3 garlic cloves, chopped
- 1 cup fresh or (thawed) frozen peas
- 1 carrot, chopped
- ¼ cup chopped fresh basil
- 4 cups cooked brown rice, for serving

Directions

1. In a steamer basket or microwave, steam the potatoes and green beans until tender. Drain and set aside.

2. In a small bowl, whisk together the coconut milk, plant-based milk, curry paste, cornstarch, maple syrup, lime juice, salt, and red pepper flakes (if using). Set aside.

3. In a large skillet, sauté the onion in a small amount of water over medium heat until tender. Add the potatoes, green beans, garlic, peas, carrot, basil, and curry mixture, turn down the heat to medium-low, and simmer for 12–15 minutes. Serve over rice.

Tips & Hints

You can use any type of potato in this recipe, but we prefer red potatoes because they are less starchy and stand up a little better in the sauce.

Tomatoes Stuffed with Pesto Rice

Pesto-stuffed tomatoes are the perfect way to use those sweet, juicy garden tomatoes. The creamy, peanutty pesto sauce has a hint of citrus and pairs perfectly with tomatoes, rice, and an assortment of fresh summer veggies. In fact, the pesto is so robust that you might find yourself adding it to pastas, potatoes, or grilled veggies.

Prep Time: 30 minutes | **Yield: 4–6 servings**

Ingredients

Pesto Sauce

1 cup fresh cilantro or basil

¼ cup all-natural peanut butter (100 percent peanuts)

¼ cup lime juice

¼ cup water

¼ cup unsweetened coconut flakes

2 teaspoons grated ginger or ginger paste

6 garlic cloves, peeled

2 jalapeño peppers, seeded and ribs removed

½ teaspoon sea salt or to taste

Vegetables and Rice

8 medium-large tomatoes

2 cups cooked brown rice

4–6 green onions, diced

1 red or orange bell pepper, seeded and diced

1 cup sliced kalamata olives

½ cup fresh or (thawed) frozen peas

¼ cup pine nuts (optional)

Directions

1. Combine all the pesto ingredients in a high-powered blender and blend until smooth and creamy. Set aside ½ cup of the pesto sauce for topping.

2. Place the tomatoes stem side down on a cutting board. Cut each tomato into 6–8 wedges, leaving the wedges attached at the base of the tomato. Carefully spread open the wedges and set the tomatoes aside.

3. In a medium bowl, combine the rice, green onions, bell pepper, olives, peas, and remaining pesto sauce and mix well.

4. Fill each tomato with the rice mixture and top with the reserved ½ cup pesto sauce and pine nuts (if using). Serve right away.

Tips & Hints

You can also bake stuffed tomatoes. Cut off the tomato tops and scoop out the pulp, leaving a ½-inch-thick shell intact. Add the pulp to the rice mixture. Stuff the tomatoes with the rice mixture and bake at 375°F for 20–25 minutes or until the tomatoes begin to shrink. Turn the oven to broil and broil until the tomato edges start to brown slightly.

Vegetable Lo Mein

Kids and adults love this healthy, oil-free version of a popular Chinese take-out dish. It's a quick and easy dinner that can be ready in under 30 minutes.

Prep Time: 15 minutes | Cook Time: 15 minutes | Yield: 4 servings

Ingredients

Sauce

¼ cup water

3 tablespoons low-sodium tamari or soy sauce

2 tablespoons pure maple syrup (or other liquid sweetener)

1 tablespoon tahini

2 teaspoons cornstarch

½–1 teaspoon sriracha

1 teaspoon garlic powder

1 teaspoon ground ginger

Lo Mein

8 ounces whole-grain spaghetti (gluten-free if necessary)

8 ounces mushrooms (any type), sliced

2 carrots, julienned

½ cup snow peas (optional)

1 red bell pepper, seeded and sliced

4–6 green onions, sliced

2–3 tablespoons sesame seeds

Directions

1. In a small bowl, whisk together all the sauce ingredients. Set aside.

2. Cook the spaghetti according to the package instructions. Drain.

3. In a large skillet, sauté the mushrooms, carrots, snow peas (if using), and bell pepper in a small amount of water over medium heat until tender, about 5 minutes.

4. Add the green onions, spaghetti, and sauce and toss to combine. Continue cooking just until the sauce begins to thicken. Serve immediately, garnished with the sesame seeds.

Instant Pot Recipes

Instant Pot Sweet Baked Beans

These simple, no-soak baked beans have the perfect balance of rich, sweet, and savory. Baked beans are the ideal accompaniment for barbecue-style dishes, veggie loaf, veggie hot dogs, or baked potatoes.

Prep Time: 30 minutes | Cook Time: 1 hour 15 minutes | Yield: 8 servings

Ingredient

1 pound dried navy beans

3 cups water

2 onions, diced

2 celery stalks, diced

2 carrots, diced

6 garlic cloves, roughly chopped

½ cup chopped dates *or* ¼ cup
　　pure maple syrup

¼ cup apple cider vinegar

¼ cup molasses

3 tablespoons tomato paste

2 tablespoons Dijon mustard

2 teaspoons liquid smoke

¼ teaspoon red pepper flakes

2 bay leaves

1 teaspoon sea salt or to taste

Directions

1. Rinse and sort the beans, removing any debris. Combine the beans, water, onions, celery, carrots, garlic, dates (or maple syrup), apple cider vinegar, molasses, tomato paste, mustard, liquid smoke, red pepper flakes, and bay leaves in the Instant Pot and stir.

2. Lock the lid into place and close the pressure valve. Cook at high pressure for 75 minutes. Once the cook time is complete, let the pressure naturally release for 8–10 minutes. Release the remaining pressure and remove the lid.

3. Remove the bay leaves and season the beans with salt. The beans will thicken as they cool.

Tips & Hints

Presoaking the beans overnight (10–12 hours) will cut down on cook time. Cook presoaked beans at high pressure for 30 minutes and let the pressure naturally release for 8–10 minutes. Release the remaining pressure and remove the lid.

Instant Pot Black Beans

I like to cook black beans for a very long time to create a creamy sauce and tender beans, and it couldn't be easier than with an Instant Pot! These black beans are great served over greens with rice and topped with salsa and guacamole. The variations are endless, and these are a staple in our household.

Prep Time: 30 minutes | Cook Time: 1 hour 15 minutes | Yield: 6 servings

Ingredients

16 ounces (2½ cups) dried black beans, rinsed

4 cups low-sodium vegetable broth

2 tablespoons lime juice

1 large onion, diced

1 poblano pepper, roughly chopped

2 tablespoons chili powder

1 teaspoon ground cumin

1 teaspoon ground coriander

1 teaspoon smoked paprika

1 teaspoon chipotle chile powder

1 teaspoon sea salt or to taste

3–5 garlic cloves, minced

Tips & Hints

Presoaking the beans overnight (10–12 hours) will cut down on cook time. Cook presoaked beans at high pressure for 30 minutes and let the pressure naturally release for 20 minutes. Release the remaining pressure and remove the lid.

Directions

1. Rinse and sort the beans, removing any debris. Combine the beans, broth, lime juice, onion, poblano pepper, chili powder, cumin, coriander, smoked paprika, chipotle powder, and salt in the Instant Pot and stir.

2. Lock the lid into place and close the pressure valve. Cook at high pressure for 75 minutes. Once the cook time is complete, let the pressure naturally release for 20 minutes. Release the remaining pressure and remove the lid. (You can also quick release the pressure.)

3. Stir in the garlic. If you prefer a thinner consistency, add more water or broth to achieve the consistency you desire. Allow the beans to cool down.

4. Using an immersion blender or a potato masher, blend or smash about half of the beans to create a creamy consistency. (This is a personal preference, but I like to see whole beans combined with a creamy texture, so I pulse 8–10 times with an immersion blender.) The beans will thicken as they cool and upon refrigeration.

Instant Pot Italian Veggie Pasta

This recipe happened because of a frantic evening when I had a limited amount of time and not much in the fridge. I had some marinara sauce, pasta, a few veggies, and pantry spices, so cooking everything together in the Instant Pot seemed like the perfect solution. The result was a vibrant, creamy pasta dish loaded with hearty veggies. We felt like we had ordered from a fancy Italian restaurant. Cooking the pasta with the marinara sauce gives this dish a unique creaminess that you simply cannot capture on the stovetop. The Instant Pot does it again!

Prep Time: 15 minutes | **Cook Time: 10 minutes** | **Yield: 4 servings**

Ingredients

1 onion, diced

1 red bell pepper, seeded and sliced

1 jalapeño pepper, seeded and small diced

2 small zucchini, large diced

4 garlic cloves, sliced

½ cup chopped fresh basil

1 pound brown rice pasta

1 (24-ounce) jar marinara sauce

3 cups water

2 teaspoons Italian seasoning

1 teaspoon sea salt or to taste

½ teaspoon black pepper

¼ teaspoon red pepper flakes

1½ cups frozen peas

4–6 ounces chopped spinach or kale

Directions

1. Using the sauté function on the Instant Pot, sauté the onion, bell pepper, and jalapeño until tender. Turn off the heat.

2. Add the zucchini, garlic, basil, pasta, marinara sauce, water, Italian seasoning, salt, black pepper, and red pepper flakes and stir.

3. Lock the lid into place and close the pressure valve. Cook at high pressure for 7 minutes. Once the cook time is complete, quick release the pressure and remove the lid.

4. Add the peas and spinach or kale and stir. Serve warm.

Instant Pot Thai Green Curry Risotto

Creamy, smooth rice infused with the flavors of Thai green curry takes the idea of risotto to a whole new level. The Instant Pot is the easiest way to pull off this meal quickly and easily, but I've included stovetop directions as well (see tip).

Prep Time: 15 minutes | **Cook Time: 15 minutes** | **Yield: 4–6 servings**

Ingredients

6–8 green onions, sliced

3 celery stalks, thinly sliced

4 garlic cloves, minced

1 jalapeño pepper, seeded, ribs removed, and thinly sliced

8 ounces mushrooms (any type), sliced

1 tablespoon grated ginger or ginger paste

2 teaspoons Thai green curry paste (such as Thai Kitchen)

1 cup cilantro, chopped, ¼ cup reserved for garnish

¼ cup chopped fresh basil

2 tablespoons white miso paste

1 cup white arborio rice

½ cup dry white wine

1½ cups frozen edamame

2 cups low-sodium vegetable broth

3 cups chopped spinach

1 lime, quartered

2 tablespoons sesame seeds, toasted (optional)

Directions

1. Using the sauté function on the Instant Pot, sauté the green onions, celery, garlic, jalapeño, mushrooms, ginger, curry paste, cilantro, and basil in a small amount of water for 3–4 minutes, stirring continuously. Add the miso paste, rice, wine, and edamame and continue to cook, stirring, for 3–4 minutes. Turn off the heat and pour in the broth.

2. Lock the lid into place and close the pressure valve. Cook at high pressure for 6 minutes. Once the cook time is complete, quick release the pressure and remove the lid.

3. Stir in the spinach. Serve immediately, garnished with the reserved cilantro, lime wedges, and sesame seeds (if using).

Tips & Hints

To cook the risotto on the stovetop, follow step 1 using a large skillet over medium-high heat. Add 2½ cups warm vegetable broth to the skillet and bring to a boil. Reduce the heat to low, cover, and cook for 20–22 minutes, stirring frequently to prevent sticking. Stir in the spinach and allow it to wilt for 5 minutes. Serve immediately, garnished as in step 3.

You can toast sesame seeds on a baking sheet at 375°F for 3–4 minutes or in a dry skillet over medium heat, stirring continuously, for 2–3 minutes. When golden and fragrant, remove them from the heat.

Instant Pot Scalloped Potatoes

As I mentioned in my Scalloped Veggies au Gratin recipe in the entrées chapter, I have always loved scalloped potatoes, and my mother makes a wonderful traditional version. Thanks, Mom! The version here speeds things up by using the Instant Pot, but the results are just as luscious.

Prep Time: 30 minutes | Cook Time: 40 minutes | Yield: 4 servings

Ingredients

Sauce

2½ cups unsweetened plant-based milk

3 tablespoons cornstarch

3 tablespoons nutritional yeast flakes

2 teaspoons lemon juice

1 teaspoon Dijon mustard

1 teaspoon garlic powder

1 teaspoon onion powder

½–¾ teaspoon salt or to taste

½ teaspoon black pepper

½ teaspoon ground turmeric

Potatoes

1½ cups water (for the bottom of the Instant Pot)

2 pounds Yukon Gold potatoes (about 4–6 medium), sliced ¼ inch thick

2 onions, halved and sliced ¼ inch thick

¼ cup chopped fresh flat-leaf parsley

¼ teaspoon smoked paprika

Directions

1. Combine all the sauce ingredients in a blender and puree until smooth.

2. Place the trivet in the Instant Pot and pour in the 1½ cups water.

3. Add a small amount of sauce to cover the bottom of each of two small insert pans (see tip). Arrange half of the potato slices and half of the onion slices in an overlapping layer in each pan. Sprinkle with parsley, then pour half of the sauce over the potatoes and onions. Repeat with the remaining potatoes, onions, parsley, and sauce. Sprinkle the smoked paprika over the top.

4. Cover the pans with aluminum foil and set the pans, stacked, on the trivet in the Instant Pot.

5. Lock the lid into place and close the pressure valve. Cook at high pressure for 35 minutes. Once the cook time is complete, quick release the pressure and remove the lid.

6. Turn on the oven broiler.

7. Carefully remove the insert pans from the Instant Pot using the trivet handles. Remove the aluminum foil and place the pans on a rimmed

baking sheet. Broil for 4–5 minutes or until the top of the potatoes are golden. Serve immediately.

Tips & Hints

I use Ekovana insert pans for my Instant Pot, but you can also use any regular round cake pans that fit inside.

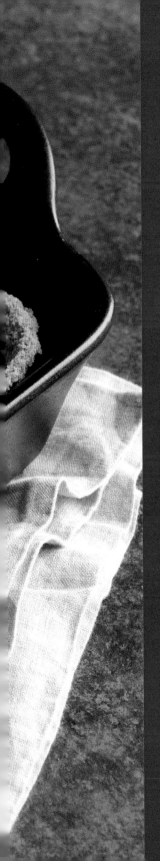

Holiday Recipes

Looking for more holiday favorites? Some other recipes for your holiday table:

Thanksgiving Green Bean Casserole

This casserole originates from a traditional recipe calling for canned mushroom soup, canned green beans, and highly processed canned fried onion rings. When I was a kid, Thanksgiving dinner was not complete without this kid-friendly casserole. Creating a healthy version was easy, and it has become special in our home because the onion rings are made in-house. The onion rings require a bit more time, but it's well worth the effort—that is, if you can manage to not eat all the onion rings before they make it to the top of the casserole!

Prep Time: 30 minutes | **Cook Time: 1 hour** | **Yield: 6 servings**

Ingredients

Onion Rings

1 cup unsweetened plant-based milk

1¼ cups whole-grain flour (gluten-free if necessary)

2 cups whole-grain bread crumbs (gluten-free if necessary)

2 tablespoons nutritional yeast flakes

1 teaspoon garlic powder

1 teaspoon onion powder

½ teaspoon sea salt or to taste

1 large white or red onion, cut into ¼-inch-thick rings

Sauce

1½ cups unsweetened plant-based milk

½ cup raw cashews

2–3 garlic cloves, peeled

2 tablespoons nutritional yeast flakes

1½ tablespoons cornstarch

2 teaspoons apple cider vinegar

1 teaspoon onion powder

½ teaspoon sea salt or to taste

½ teaspoon black pepper

¼ teaspoon ground nutmeg

Veggies

12 ounces mushrooms (any type), sliced or chopped

2–3 tablespoons dry white wine

1 (24-ounce) package frozen French-cut or whole green beans, thawed

Directions

1. Preheat the oven to 425°F. Line a rimmed baking sheet with parchment paper or a silicone mat.

2. Line up three shallow bowls. In the first bowl, put the milk. In the second bowl, put the flour. In the third bowl, combine the bread crumbs, nutritional yeast, garlic powder, onion powder, and salt (optional).

3. Coat the onion rings first in the flour, then in the milk, and then in the bread crumb mixture. You can do several onion rings at once.

4. Place the breaded onion rings on the lined baking sheet. Bake for 10–15 minutes or until golden brown and crispy. Turn the oven temperature down to 375°F.

5. Meanwhile, combine all the sauce ingredients in a high-powered blender and blend until smooth and creamy. Set aside.

6. In a large skillet, sauté the mushrooms in the wine over medium-high heat for 6–8 minutes or until tender.

7. Transfer the mushrooms to a 9 × 13-inch baking pan and mix in the green beans. Pour the sauce over the vegetables, distributing it evenly. Top the casserole with the baked onion rings and cover with aluminum foil. Bake for 30 minutes. Remove the foil and continue to bake for an additional 20 minutes or until golden brown and crispy.

Marinated Carrot
Salad (page 139)

Cranberry Orange Roasted
Brussel Sprouts (page 138)

Holiday Nut Loaf

Holiday Nut Loaf GF

This classic hearty loaf is loaded with flavor and great textures. The nuts really make it special, so it's a perfect centerpiece for the holidays. To make the recipe quick and easy, I use store-bought barbecue sauce for the glaze. Serve with mashed potatoes and mushroom gravy.

Prep Time: 20 minutes | Cook Time: 55 minutes | Yield: 6 servings

Ingredients

1 cup walnuts

1 cup raw almonds

1 cup rolled oats (not quick oats; gluten-free if necessary)

1 (15-ounce) can chickpeas, drained (liquid reserved) and rinsed

1 onion, diced

2 celery stalks, finely diced

4–5 garlic cloves, minced

1 (6-ounce) can tomato paste

2 tablespoons vegan Worcestershire sauce

½ teaspoon liquid smoke

¼ cup nutritional yeast flakes

2 teaspoons Italian seasoning

1 teaspoon poultry seasoning

½ teaspoon sea salt or to taste

½ teaspoon black pepper

1½ cups oil-free barbecue sauce (such as Bone Suckin' Sauce)

Tips & Hints

You can make a smaller loaf and then use the leftover mixture to make veggie patties or veggie balls.

Directions

1. Preheat the oven to 375°F. Line a 9 × 5-inch loaf pan with parchment paper.

2. Combine the walnuts, almonds, and oats in a food processor and process until coarsely ground. Add the chickpeas and pulse until they are coarsely ground but not mushy. Transfer the mixture to a large bowl.

3. Add 2 tablespoons of the reserved chickpea liquid (aka aquafaba), the onion, celery, garlic, tomato paste, Worcestershire sauce, liquid smoke, nutritional yeast, Italian seasoning, poultry seasoning, salt, and pepper to the chickpea mixture. Stir well, making sure to incorporate everything.

4. Transfer the mixture to the lined loaf pan, packing it into the corners and smoothing the top. Spread half of the barbecue sauce evenly over the top. Cover with aluminum foil and bake for 30 minutes. Remove the foil, pour the remaining barbecue sauce over the loaf, and continue baking for 20–25 minutes or until the glaze is caramelized and slightly dry to the touch. Allow the loaf to cool for 15 minutes before slicing.

DIY Mason Jar Edible Gifts

(Split Pea Lentil Soup Jar, Blueberry Gingerbread Pancake Jar, Muesli Jar)

Are you looking for a gift for someone but feeling overwhelmed? Homemade mason jar recipes are economical, quick, easy to assemble, and a fun way to show someone you care. They're also an excellent activity for kids. I've included a few of my favorites, but don't be afraid to be creative and develop your own recipes. I recommend choosing recipes that contain a variety of mainly dry ingredients so you can layer them in a jar. Make sure to include the directions for cooking. These jars are perfect for holidays, birthdays, baby and bridal showers, party favors, and more.

Split Pea Lentil Soup Jar

Prep Time: 10 minutes | Cook Time: 18 minutes (Instant Pot), 2 hours (stovetop), or 4 hours (slow cooker) | Yield: 4 servings

Ingredients

¼ cup farro or barley

½ cup dried split peas

¼ cup brown rice

½ cup dried green lentils

Spice Packet

2 tablespoons dried minced onion

1 tablespoon dried parsley

1 teaspoon Italian seasoning

1 teaspoon garlic powder

½ teaspoon sea salt or to taste

½ teaspoon black pepper

½ teaspoon dried sage

¼ teaspoon ground cumin

Directions for assembling the mason jar

1. Using a funnel, put the farro or barley, split peas, rice, and lentils in a pint-size mason jar in the order listed, creating layers.

2. Combine all the spices in a snack-size zip-top plastic bag and carefully fit it in the top of the jar.

3. Close the lid, decorate, and label creatively. Be sure to include the directions (below) for preparing the soup.

Directions for preparing the soup

1. Set aside the spice packet. Empty the remaining mason jar contents into a colander and rinse well.

2. To cook the soup, you have a choice of methods:

- **Stovetop:** Combine the rinsed ingredients in a large pot and add the spices. Cover with 5 cups water. Add 2–3 diced carrots and 2 diced celery stalks. Bring to a boil, then lower the heat to medium-low and simmer for 2 hours, stirring occasionally. If you prefer a thinner soup, simply add more water.

- **Slow cooker:** Combine the rinsed ingredients in a slow cooker and add the spices. Cover with 5 cups water. Add 2–3 diced carrots and 2 diced celery stalks. Cover and cook on high for 4 hours.

- **Instant Pot:** Combine the rinsed ingredients in the Instant Pot and add the spices. Cover with 4 cups water. Add 2–3 diced carrots and 2 diced celery stalks. Lock the lid into place and close the pressure valve. Cook at high pressure for 18 minutes. Once the cook time is complete, quick release the pressure and remove the lid.

Blueberry Gingerbread Pancake Jar

Prep Time: 5 minutes | Cook Time: 15 minutes | Yield: 8–10 pancakes

Ingredients

1½ cups white whole-wheat flour (or oat flour for gluten-free)

1 tablespoon coconut sugar

1½ teaspoons baking powder

1 teaspoon ground cinnamon

¼ teaspoon ground cloves

½ teaspoon ground ginger

¼ teaspoon nutmeg

¼ teaspoon sea salt

½ cup dried blueberries

Directions for assembling the mason jar

1. In a large bowl, whisk together the flour, coconut sugar, baking powder, cinnamon, cloves, ginger, nutmeg, and salt.

2. Using a funnel, put half of the flour mixture in a pint-size mason jar. Add the dried blueberries and then the remaining flour mixture.

3. Close the lid, decorate, and label creatively. Be sure to include the following directions for preparing the pancakes.

Directions for preparing the pancakes

1. Preheat a griddle over medium heat for 5 minutes.

2. In a medium bowl, whisk together 1¾ cups unsweetened plant-based milk and 2 tablespoons molasses.

3. Add the mason jar contents to the bowl and mix just until combined; do not overmix. You will have some lumps, but that's fine. For thicker or thinner pancakes, simply adjust the milk.

4. Drop ¼–½ cup of batter per pancake onto the preheated griddle. Cook until bubbles appear in the middle of the pancakes. Flip and continue cooking for 2–3 minutes. Repeat to make all the pancakes.

Muesli Jar

Prep Time: 5 minutes | Yield: 7¼ cups

Ingredients

3 cups rolled oats (not quick oats)

1 cup wheat or bran flakes

1 cup puffed millet, rice, Kamut, or corn cereal (such as Arrowhead Mills)

1 cup raisins, dried blueberries, or dried cranberries

½ cup chopped dates

¼ cup unsweetened coconut flakes

¼ cup sunflower seeds

¼ cup pumpkin seeds

3 tablespoons flax meal

1 tablespoon ground cinnamon

Directions

1. Combine all the ingredients in a large bowl and mix well.

2. Using a funnel, transfer the ingredients to three pint-size jars.

3. Close the lid, decorate, and label creatively.

Scalloped Corn

We always serve scalloped corn at Thanksgiving. It's simple to prepare and always the first dish that is devoured. The recipe has no added sugars, but the corn gives the dish a mildly sweet yet savory flavor.

Prep Time: 15 minutes | **Cook Time: 35 minutes** | **Yield: 6 servings**

Ingredients

1 onion, diced

2 green bell peppers, seeded and diced

¼ cup low-sodium vegetable broth

2 cups unsweetened plant-based milk

6 tablespoons whole-wheat flour (or oat flour for gluten-free)

½ teaspoon ground mustard

½ teaspoon black pepper

½ teaspoon smoked or regular paprika

⅛ teaspoon ground nutmeg

6 cups fresh or (thawed) frozen corn

¼ cup whole-grain bread crumbs (gluten-free if necessary)

Directions

1. Preheat the oven to 375°F.

2. In a large skillet, sauté the onion and bell peppers in the broth over high heat until tender.

3. In a large bowl, whisk together the milk, flour, mustard, black pepper, paprika, and nutmeg until completely smooth.

4. Add the corn and sautéed onion and peppers to the bowl and mix well. Transfer the mixture to a 9-inch square baking pan. Sprinkle with the bread crumbs and bake for 30 minutes or until the top is bubbly and golden brown.

Sugar Cookie Cutouts

Christmas cookies have always been part of our family tradition. As I've worked on creating a healthier version over the years, I have found that walnuts and applesauce make an excellent fat replacer and create a soft and fluffy cookie.

Prep Time: 30 minutes, plus 1–2 hours chilling time |
Cook Time: 6–9 minutes | Yield: 25–30 cookies

Ingredients

Cookies

¼ cup unsweetened plant-based milk

¼ cup unsweetened applesauce

¼ cup pure maple syrup (or other liquid sweetener)

¼ cup walnuts

1 teaspoon almond extract

2 cups whole-wheat pastry flour, plus more for dusting

¼ cup coconut sugar

1½ teaspoons baking powder

½ teaspoon ground cinnamon

¼ teaspoon sea salt

Frosting and Decorations

1½ cups confectioners' sugar

5–6 teaspoons unsweetened plant-based milk, plus more as needed

½ teaspoon pure vanilla extract or almond extract

Food coloring (optional)

Unsweetened coconut flakes, raisins, nuts, seeds, and/or cacao nibs, for decorating

Directions

1. Preheat the oven to 375°F. Line two rimmed baking sheets with parchment paper or silicone mats.

2. Combine the milk, applesauce, maple syrup, walnuts, and almond extract in a high-powered blender and blend until smooth and creamy.

3. In a large bowl, whisk together the flour, coconut sugar, baking powder, cinnamon, and salt.

4. Pour the wet ingredients into the dry ingredients and mix just until a large dough ball forms; do not knead or overmix the dough. Wrap the dough ball in plastic wrap and refrigerate for 1–2 hours.

5. Dust a work surface with flour. Place half of the dough ball on the surface and sprinkle some flour over the top of the dough. With a rolling pin, roll out the dough to a ¼-inch thickness, adding more flour as needed if the dough starts to stick. Cut into shapes with your favorite cookie cutters. Repeat with the other half of the dough ball.

6. Transfer the cookies to the lined baking sheets. Bake for 6–9 minutes or lightly browned. Allow the cookies to cool completely on wire racks before frosting.

7. When ready to frost the cookies, whisk together the confectioners' sugar, milk, and vanilla or almond extract. Stir in extra milk, a teaspoon at a time, if you prefer a thinner consistency. If you want to dye your frosting, divide the frosting into separate bowls and add a few drops of food coloring to each bowl, stirring until the desired shade is reached. Frost and decorate your cookies however you like.

Sugar Cookie
Cutouts

Thumbprint Cookies (page 252)

No-Bake Coconut Pumpkin Pie

Thanksgiving is the one time of year I wish I had two ovens. We love this no-bake pumpkin pie filling because it's one less oven project and is every bit as rich and decadent as the filling in those traditional pumpkin pies we all grew up on.

Prep Time: 20 minutes, plus 3–4 hours chilling time | Yield: 8–10 servings

Ingredients

Crust

1½ cups rolled oats (not quick oats; gluten-free if necessary)

1 cup walnuts

1 cup pitted dates, soaked

2 tablespoons unsweetened applesauce

2 teaspoons pure vanilla extract

1 teaspoon pumpkin pie spice, store-bought or homemade (page 67)

Filling

1 (14-ounce) package extra-firm tofu, drained

1 (15-ounce) can pumpkin puree

1 cup canned lite coconut milk

½ cup pure maple syrup (or other liquid sweetener)

2 teaspoons pure vanilla extract

1 tablespoon pumpkin pie spice, store-bought or homemade (page 67)

½ teaspoon sea salt

¾ cup water

4 teaspoons agar-agar powder (not flakes)

Topping

½ cup vegan chocolate chips

Directions

1. In a food processor, pulse all the crust ingredients. Press the mixture into a 9-inch pie plate.

2. Combine the tofu, pumpkin, coconut milk, maple syrup, vanilla, pumpkin pie spice, and salt in a blender and blend until smooth and creamy.

3. Pour the water into a small saucepan, sprinkle the agar-agar powder into the water, and whisk. Bring the mixture to a boil, then reduce the heat and gently simmer for 1–2 minutes, whisking continuously. Pour the agar mixture into the blender with the pumpkin mixture and blend for 1 minute.

4. Pour the pumpkin filling mixture over the crust, then refrigerate until firm and set, 3–4 hours.

5. When you are ready to serve the pie, melt the chocolate chips in a small bowl in the microwave for 1–2 minutes. Serve the pie chilled or at room temperature, with the melted chocolate drizzled over the top.

Tips & Hints

Agar-agar is a plant-based gelatin found in most Asian markets, natural food stores, and online. There is a big difference between agar-agar flakes and powder, so stick with the powder for this recipe.

Cornbread Dressing with Cranberries

This old-fashioned southern-style cornbread dressing is oil-free but still moist and is deliciously flavored with sage, thyme, rosemary, onion, and celery. The cranberries give it a refreshing burst of color and flavor.

Prep Time: 30 minutes | Cook Time: 50 minutes | Yield: 6–8 servings

Ingredients

- 6 cups cubed cornbread
- 1 cup water
- ½ cup raw cashews
- 1¾ cups low-sodium vegetable broth
- 2 tablespoons flax meal
- 4 celery stalks, diced
- 1 large onion, diced
- ½ cup chopped pecans or walnuts
- ½ cup chopped fresh flat-leaf parsley
- 2 tablespoons chopped fresh thyme
- 1 tablespoon chopped fresh sage
- 1 tablespoon chopped fresh rosemary
- 1 teaspoon fennel seeds, toasted
- ¼ teaspoon red pepper flakes
- ½ cup fresh cranberries
- 1 teaspoon sea salt or to taste
- ¼ teaspoon black pepper

Directions

1. Preheat the oven to 350°F. Line a 9 × 13-inch baking pan with parchment paper.

2. Spread out the cornbread cubes in a single layer on a rimmed baking sheet. Bake for 10–15 minutes or until golden.

3. Meanwhile, combine the water and cashews in a high-powered blender and blend until smooth. Transfer the cashew cream to a medium bowl, add the broth and flax meal, and whisk well. Set aside.

4. In a large skillet, sauté the celery and onion in a small amount of water over medium-high heat until the onion is translucent. Stir in the pecans or walnuts, parsley, thyme, sage, rosemary, fennel seeds, red pepper flakes, and cranberries.

5. Transfer the vegetable mixture to a large bowl. Add the toasted cornbread cubes, season with the salt and pepper, and gently toss to combine. Pour the cashew cream mixture over the cornbread mixture and toss gently.

6. Spread the stuffing into the lined baking pan, cover with aluminum foil, and bake for 30 minutes. Remove the foil and continue baking for another 10–15 minutes or until golden.

On the
Sweeter Side

Boston Cream Pie

Boston cream pie isn't really a pie; it's more like an éclair—a deliciously moist vanilla cake with pudding in the middle, topped with chocolate ganache. This cake was part of a love story that started in 1981. My husband and I met when we were sixteen years old; two years later, I took a gourmet cooking class where I experimented with a Boston cream pie. I had a lot of leftovers to share, so Nelson became my official tester. He repeatedly requested that treat, which I continued to make for him—especially because I knew he was the perfect catch. Thirty-eight years later, I have finally come up with a delicious plant-based and oil-free version that is significantly healthier than my earliest rendition. Sandwiched between the cake layers is a simple vanilla pudding, and on top of the cake is a sweet potato chocolate icing.

Prep Time: 40 minutes | **Cook Time: 35 minutes** | **Yield: 10 servings**

Ingredients

Cake

2 cups superfine almond flour (not almond meal)

1 cup white rice flour

¾ cup coconut sugar

½ cup potato starch

½ cup tapioca starch

4 teaspoons baking powder

½ teaspoon sea salt

1½ cups unsweetened plant-based milk

½ cup unsweetened applesauce

¼ cup aquafaba (liquid from canned chickpeas)

1½ tablespoons apple cider vinegar

1 tablespoon pure vanilla extract

Pudding

1¾ cups unsweetened plant-based milk

3–4 tablespoons pure maple syrup (or other liquid sweetener)

3 tablespoons cornstarch

⅛ teaspoon ground turmeric (optional, for color)

⅛ teaspoon sea salt

2 teaspoons pure vanilla extract

Sweet Potato Chocolate Ganache

⅓ cup vegan chocolate chips

1 cup mashed cooked sweet potatoes

½ cup unsweetened cocoa powder

5 tablespoons canned lite coconut milk

3 tablespoons pure maple syrup (or other liquid sweetener)

1 teaspoon pure vanilla extract

Directions

1. Preheat the oven to 350°F. Line a 9-inch springform pan or regular cake pan with parchment paper.

2. First, make the cake. In a large bowl, whisk together the almond flour, rice flour, coconut sugar, potato starch, tapioca starch, baking powder, and salt. In a medium bowl, whisk together the milk, applesauce, aquafaba, vinegar, and vanilla. Pour the wet ingredients into the dry ingredients and mix with a handheld mixer for 1–2 minutes.

3. Pour the batter into the lined pan and bake for 30 minutes or until a toothpick inserted in the center comes out clean. Allow the cake to cool for about 10 minutes, then run a thin knife around the edges to release the cake from the pan. Open the latch and remove the sides. Transfer the cake to a wire rack to cool for 90 minutes. It is very important to cool the cake fully before adding the pudding. Otherwise, the cake won't split easily and can develop a gummy, sticky texture.

4. Meanwhile, make the pudding. In a small saucepan, whisk together the milk, maple syrup, cornstarch, turmeric (if using), and salt until the cornstarch is completely dissolved. Turn the heat to medium-high and bring the mixture to a boil, whisking continuously. Once the mixture boils, reduce the heat to medium-low and continue whisking for 2 minutes. Turn off the heat and add the vanilla. Cover and set aside.

5. To make the ganache, first melt the chocolate chips in a small bowl in the microwave for 1–2 minutes. Combine the sweet potatoes, cocoa powder, coconut milk, maple syrup, and vanilla in a high-powered blender and blend until smooth and creamy. Add the melted chocolate and blend for another 30 seconds.

6. Carefully cut the cake in half through the middle (see tip). Place the bottom layer of the cake, cut side up, on a serving plate. Spread the pudding over the bottom layer, then top with the top layer of the cake, cut side down. Finally, spread the ganache over the top of the cake. Cover and refrigerate until ready to serve.

Tips & Hints

You can substitute 2 cups gluten-free flour for the rice flour, potato starch, and tapioca starch.

To make it easier to cut the cake in half, place toothpicks all around the perimeter at the halfway mark and cut with a long serrated knife, using a sawing motion.

Old-Fashioned Fig Roll Cookies

Fig Newtons are a classic cookie from the past, but these reinterpreted gems are much healthier and tastier than anything you will find in a store. In these bars, delicious gluten-free cookie dough is layered with a thick, rich, jammy fig puree, a perfect pairing. Figs are honey sweet and have a unique, slightly berry-like flavor that makes these cookies almost magical. They're great as a breakfast, snack, or dessert.

Prep Time: 30 minutes | Cook Time: 8–10 minutes | Yield: 16–18 cookies

Ingredients

Filling

6 ounces dried Turkish or Black Mission figs

1 tablespoon lemon juice

1 teaspoon pure vanilla extract

Pinch of sea salt

Dough

1 cup superfine almond flour (not almond meal)

1 cup oat flour, plus more as needed

1 tablespoon flax meal

1 tablespoon tapioca starch

1 teaspoon baking powder

¼ cup unsweetened applesauce

2 tablespoons pure maple syrup (or other liquid sweetener)

1 teaspoon pure vanilla extract

Directions

1. Preheat the oven to 350°F. Line a rimmed baking sheet with parchment paper or a silicone mat.

2. Put the dried figs in a bowl and cover them with boiling water. Allow them to soak for 10–12 minutes. Drain and set aside.

3. Meanwhile, make the cookie dough. In a medium bowl, whisk together the almond flour, oat flour, flax meal, tapioca starch, and baking powder until thoroughly combined. Add the applesauce, maple syrup, and vanilla. Stir until the ingredients are combined and the dough is thick enough to be formed into a ball. Divide the dough in half. (If the dough is too sticky, add a bit more oat flour to the dough or chill the dough for 1–2 hours.)

4. To make the filling, put the drained figs, lemon juice, vanilla, and salt in a food processor. Start pulsing to break up the figs, then process for 8–10 seconds or until a thick paste forms.

5. Place one ball of dough on a sheet of parchment paper and shape it into a log. Lay another sheet of

parchment over the log and use a rolling pin to roll the dough into a 12 × 4-inch rectangle about ¼ inch thick. Remove the top parchment and use your hands to form an even rectangle. Spoon half of the fig paste down the center of the dough. Lift one long side of the parchment paper and fold the dough up and over the fig filling until the two dough edges close. Remove the parchment and shape and slightly flatten the roll, then slice into 1–1½-inch cookies. Place the cookies on the lined baking sheet. Repeat with the remaining cookie dough and fig paste. Bake for 8–10 minutes or until slightly golden.

Tips & Hints

If you prefer a grasshopper pie, simply assemble the recipe on a parchment-lined pie plate.

You can turn the mint filling into a chocolate-mint filling by adding ¼ cup unsweetened cocoa powder.

Grasshopper Bars

These beautiful and decadent layered bars are a mint chocolate bomb! They are loaded with the flavors of chocolate and mint, which are paired with the creamy texture of ripe avocado and banana.

Prep Time: 20 minutes, plus 6–8 hours freezing time |
Cook Time: 1–2 minutes | Yield: 8 servings

Ingredients

Crust

1 cup rolled oats (not quick oats; gluten-free if necessary)

½ cup walnuts

10–12 pitted dates, soaked

¼ cup unsweetened cocoa powder

1 teaspoon peppermint extract

Pinch of sea salt

2–3 tablespoons water

Filling

2 medium ripe avocados, pitted and peeled

1 banana

½ cup pure maple syrup (or other liquid sweetener)

2 tablespoons crème de menthe

1 tablespoon lemon juice

½ teaspoon peppermint extract

Topping

½ cup vegan chocolate chips

¼ cup cacao nibs

Directions

1. Line an 8-inch square baking pan with parchment paper.

2. Combine the oats, walnuts, dates, cocoa powder, peppermint extract, and salt in a food processor and process until you have a grainy mixture. Add the water, 1 tablespoon at a time, until the mixture has a sticky consistency and will hold together for a crust. Be careful not to make the mixture too wet; add just enough water so that it begins to stick together. Transfer the mixture to the lined baking pan. Evenly spread and press the crust mixture so the entire pan is covered.

3. Combine all the filling ingredients in a high-powered blender and blend until you have a smooth texture, much like frosting. Spread the filling mixture over the crust. Place the pan in the freezer for 6–8 hours or until completely frozen.

4. Melt the chocolate chips in a small bowl in the microwave for 1–2 minutes. Pour the melted chocolate over the filling mixture and spread evenly. Garnish with the cacao nibs. Place the pan back in the freezer for 30 minutes to let the chocolate set. Cut into 12–16 bars. Store in the freezer and serve cold.

Key Lime Avocado Pie

This refreshingly sweet and tart tropical dessert wins over everyone's taste buds, and it's so easy to make! It has no cream, no eggs, no butter, and no processed graham crackers—just a creamy tart and sweet lime pudding sitting atop a walnut and oat crust. Fresh avocados with a splash of coconut milk are the secret to this much-loved update to the traditional recipe.

Prep Time: 30 minutes, plus 1–2 hours freezing time | Yield: 8 servings

Ingredients

Crust

1 cup pitted dates, soaked

1 cup walnuts

1 cup rolled oats (not quick oats)

½ cup unsweetened coconut flakes

1 teaspoon pure vanilla extract

Filling

4 avocados, pitted and peeled

Grated zest of 2 limes (preferably key limes)

½ cup lime juice (preferably from key limes)

¼ cup canned full-fat coconut milk

¾ cup pure maple syrup (or other liquid sweetener)

Garnish

2–3 tablespoons unsweetened coconut flakes

1 lime (preferably a key lime), thinly sliced

Directions

1. Pulse all the crust ingredients in a food processor until a coarse meal forms and starts to come together. Press the crust mixture into a 9-inch tart pan or pie plate.

2. Combine all the filling ingredients in a high-powered blender and blend until smooth and creamy. The filling should have a pudding-like texture.

3. Pour the filling into the crust and spread evenly. Place the pie in the freezer for 1–2 hours or until firm, then decorate with the coconut flakes and lime slices. Slice and serve cold. Store the pie in the freezer or refrigerator.

> **Tips & Hints**
>
> *You can also pour the filling mixture into ice pop molds to create refreshing key lime ice pops.*

Lemon Bars GF

These delicious lemon bars have a secret ingredient: beautiful Japanese sweet potatoes! These frozen delights are creamy, sweet, and loaded with fresh lemon and coconut flavors.

Prep Time: 20 minutes, plus 3–4 hours freezing time |
Cook Time: 15 minutes | Yield: 6–8 servings

Ingredients

2 large Japanese sweet potatoes (about 1 pound each), peeled and roughly chopped

1 cup rolled oats (not quick oats; gluten-free if necessary)

¾ cup walnuts

¾ cup unsweetened coconut flakes, divided

½ cup pitted dates, soaked

2 teaspoons lemon extract

1 teaspoon ground cinnamon

2 tablespoons unsweetened applesauce

1 (13-ounce) can lite coconut milk

½ cup pure maple syrup (or other liquid sweetener)

Grated zest of 1 lemon

¼ cup lemon juice

Directions

1. Bring a medium saucepan of water to a boil. Add the sweet potatoes and boil for 15 minutes or until tender when pierced with a fork. Drain and let cool.

2. Line an 8-inch square baking pan with parchment paper.

3. Combine the oats, walnuts, ½ cup of the coconut flakes, dates, lemon extract, and cinnamon in a food processor and pulse until the mixture is finely ground and has a sticky consistency. Add the applesauce and continue pulsing until the mixture sticks together. Press the mixture evenly into the lined baking pan.

4. Combine the sweet potatoes, coconut milk, maple syrup, and lemon zest and juice in the food processor and process until creamy and smooth.

5. Spread the filling over the crust and smooth the top. Place in the freezer for 3–4 hours or until completely frozen. Remove from the freezer and allow to thaw for 15–20 minutes. Sprinkle the remaining ¼ cup coconut flakes over the top. Cut into bars and serve. Store leftover bars in the freezer.

No-Bake Berry Cheesecake

Everyone loves a traditional all-American cheesecake, and this dairy-free cake is delicate, beautiful, and delicious. The base is made with cashews, but the structure comes from agar-agar, a plant-based gelatin derived from seaweed. We love to make this dessert during blueberry season, but feel free to try it any season of the year with frozen blueberries or any of your favorite berries.

Prep Time: 20 minutes, plus 1–2 hours chilling time | Cook Time: 8 minutes | Yield: 8–10 servings

Ingredients

Berry Jam

1½ cups fresh or frozen berries

2 tablespoons chia seeds

1 tablespoon pure maple syrup (or other liquid sweetener)

1 tablespoon lemon juice

Crust

1 cup walnuts

1 cup rolled oats (not quick oats; gluten-free if necessary)

½ cup pitted dates, soaked

½ cup unsweetened coconut flakes

Pie Filling

2 cups fresh or frozen berries

1½ cups raw cashews

1 (13-ounce) can full-fat coconut milk

Grated zest and juice of ½ lemon

2 teaspoons cornstarch

2 teaspoons agar-agar powder (not flakes)

1 teaspoon pure vanilla extract

Pinch of sea salt

Directions

1. Combine all the berry jam ingredients in a small saucepan and cook over medium-high heat for 2–3 minutes or until the mixture becomes bubbly and the berries begin to break down (you can use a fork or potato masher to help break down the berries). Transfer the jam to a small bowl and set aside to cool; when cool, place in the refrigerator to thicken.

2. Meanwhile, line an 8-inch springform pan with parchment paper.

3. Combine all the crust ingredients in a food processor and process until the mixture has a sticky consistency and holds together. Transfer the crust mixture to the lined springform pan. Evenly press the mixture so it covers the entire pan. Set aside.

4. Combine all the filling ingredients in a high-powered blender and blend until smooth and creamy.

5. Pour the filling mixture into a saucepan and cook over medium-high heat until it begins to bubble. Reduce the heat to medium and cook, stirring continuously, for 3 more minutes. The mixture will become thick and bubbly.

6. Pour the filling mixture over the piecrust. Place the pie in the refrigerator for 1–2 hours to set. Remove the pie from the springform pan, slice, and top each serving with a spoonful of berry jam.

Peanut Butter Cup Bars GF

Gather round, peanut butter and chocolate lovers, because these two ingredients are the star of this ridiculously delicious and easy no-bake dessert bar! These treats have only five ingredients, but they combine to create a rich, creamy, and delicious dessert.

Prep Time: 10 minutes, plus 2 hours chilling time | Yield: 6–8 servings

Ingredients

- 1½ cups rolled oats (not quick oats; gluten-free if necessary)
- 1 cup pitted dates, soaked
- 1 cup all-natural peanut butter (100 percent peanuts), divided
- ½ cup peanuts
- 1 cup vegan chocolate chips

Directions

1. Line a 9-inch square baking pan with parchment paper. Set aside.

2. In a food processor, process the oats and dates until you have a crumbly mixture. Add ½ cup of the peanut butter and the peanuts and pulse until the mixture holds together when shaped by your hands. Press and smooth the mixture into an even layer in the lined baking pan.

3. Put the chocolate chips and remaining ½ cup peanut butter in a small bowl and microwave in 30-second intervals until melted. Mix the melted peanut butter and chocolate until thoroughly combined and pour the chocolate sauce over the peanut base.

4. Place the pan in the refrigerator for 2 hours (or in the freezer for 1 hour) or until set.

5. Cut into 12–16 bars and store in the refrigerator or freezer.

Raw Energy Bites

Dates, oats, and walnuts are the perfect start to any raw cookie or bar. It's easy to customize these delicious bites according to what you have on hand and your taste preferences. These are excellent snacks for traveling, lunch boxes, and even a quick grab-and-go breakfast.

Prep Time: 15 minutes | Yield: 15 bites

Ingredients

1 cup rolled oats (not quick oats; gluten-free if necessary)

¼ cup quinoa, toasted

½ cup walnuts

½ cup pitted dates, soaked

¼ cup flax meal

2 tablespoons sesame seeds

1 tablespoon unsweetened applesauce

1 teaspoon pure vanilla extract

1 teaspoon ground cinnamon

¼ teaspoon sea salt

½ cup raisins, vegan chocolate chips, and/or cacao nibs (optional)

Directions

1. Combine the oats, quinoa, walnuts, and dates in a food processor and process until crumbly and slightly moist. Add the flax meal, sesame seeds, applesauce, vanilla, cinnamon, and salt and process until a sticky dough forms that can be shaped into small balls.

2. Transfer the dough to a large bowl and mix in the raisins, chocolate chips, and/or cacao nibs (if using). Form the mixture into 15 small balls. Store in an airtight container in the refrigerator for up to 1 week or in the freezer for 1–2 months.

Tips & Hints

You can toast quinoa on a baking sheet at 375°F for 3–4 minutes or in a dry skillet over medium heat, stirring continuously, for 2–3 minutes. When golden and fragrant, remove them from the heat.

The base of these raw power nuggets is always the same, but you can change the vanilla extract to another flavor, such as almond, lemon, blueberry, or maple extract. Or try adding some unsweetened coconut flakes and unsweetened cocoa powder to make chocolate-coconut energy bites.

Sweet Potato Chocolate Pudding Pie ⟨GF⟩

Sweet potatoes have a starchy sweetness that makes them the ideal complement to chocolate, and together they form the perfect base for a decadent, sweet, and creamy dessert. For a nut-free version, try it without the crust, as a pudding, parfait, or ice pop.

Prep Time: 30 minutes, plus 1–2 hours chilling time | Yield: 10–12 servings

Ingredients

Crust

1 cup rolled oats (not quick oats; gluten-free if necessary)

1 cup walnuts

1 cup pitted dates

½ cup unsweetened coconut flakes (optional)

½ teaspoon ground cinnamon

1–2 tablespoons unsweetened applesauce or unsweetened plant-based milk, plus more as needed

Filling

4 cups mashed cooked sweet potatoes

1 cup pitted dates, soaked

⅔ cup unsweetened plant-based milk, plus more as needed

½ cup unsweetened cocoa powder

2 teaspoons pure vanilla extract

¼ teaspoon sea salt

½ cup vegan chocolate chips

Directions

1. Combine the oats, walnuts, dates, coconut flakes (if using), and cinnamon in a food processor and process until you achieve a grainy consistency. The mixture will feel slightly sticky.

2. Add the applesauce or milk, 1 tablespoon at a time, and pulse a few times. The mixture will become less grainy and stick together more. You should be able to squeeze the dough with your fingers to mold it into any shape. If it feels too dry, add more applesauce or milk.

3. Press the crust mixture into the bottom and sides of a 9-inch pie plate or springform pan. Set aside.

4. Combine the sweet potatoes, dates, milk, cocoa powder, vanilla, and salt in a blender and blend on high until very smooth. If necessary, you can add a little more milk if you are having trouble blending the mixture. It may take a while, and you may need to periodically stop the blender and scrape the mixture down the sides with a spatula. The final product should be smooth and creamy.

5. Meanwhile, melt the chocolate chips in a small bowl in the microwave for 1–2 minutes. Add the melted chocolate to the blender and continue blending on high.

6. Pour the mixture into the piecrust and smooth out the surface. Place the pie in the refrigerator for 1–2 hours or until firm to the touch. Cut and serve cold.

Tips & Hints

You can use a food processor instead of a blender for the filling, but you may not get quite as smooth of a consistency.

The chocolate chips are what make this pie firm up when refrigerated, so don't even consider leaving them out!

Sweet Potato Fudge Brownies

These irresistible fudgy, sweet, dense brownies owe their decadence to sweet potatoes and avocado—and, of course, chocolate! The center of the brownie is rich and moist like in a traditional brownie, but these are made without oil and eggs. Put them in the freezer so you can have a treat anytime.

Prep Time: 15 minutes | **Cook Time: 30 minutes** | **Yield: 8–12 servings**

Ingredients

- 2 tablespoons flax meal
- 6 tablespoons water
- ¾ cup white whole-wheat flour (or oat flour for gluten-free)
- ⅓ cup unsweetened cocoa powder
- 1 teaspoon baking powder
- ¼ teaspoon sea salt
- ½–¾ cup vegan chocolate chips
- 1 avocado, pitted and peeled
- 1 cup mashed cooked sweet potatoes
- ½ cup coconut sugar
- ¼ cup pure maple syrup (or other liquid sweetener)
- ¼ cup unsweetened plant-based milk
- 2 teaspoons pure vanilla extract

Directions

1. Preheat the oven to 375°F. Line a 9-inch square baking pan with parchment paper.

2. In a small bowl, whisk together the flax meal and water to make a flax "egg." Let stand for 2 minutes.

3. In a medium bowl, whisk together the flour, cocoa powder, baking powder, and salt. Add the chocolate chips and mix well.

4. In a blender, combine the avocado, sweet potatoes, coconut sugar, maple syrup, milk, and vanilla and blend until smooth and creamy. Pour the mixture into the bowl with the dry ingredients. Add the flax "egg." Stir just until the ingredients are thoroughly combined; do not overmix.

5. Spoon the batter into the lined baking pan and bake for 30–35 minutes or until the brownies are set and a toothpick inserted in the center comes out almost clean. Allow the brownies to cool completely, about 25–30 minutes, on a wire rack before slicing; this will allow you to make clean and even cuts.

Thumbprint Cookies

Thumbprint cookies are Santa's favorite cookie in our house! We love to make these moist and nutty cookies with our favorite fillings: jam, chocolate chips, or peanut butter. So use your thumb and creativity to make these fun and simple cookies that are sure to be a hit.

Prep Time: 20 minutes | Cook Time: 8–10 minutes | Yield: 18–20 cookies

Ingredients

1¾ cups oat flour (gluten-free if necessary)

⅔ cup superfine almond flour (not almond meal)

2 tablespoons tapioca starch

1 teaspoon baking powder

¼ teaspoon sea salt

½ cup coconut sugar

½ cup unsweetened applesauce

¼ cup all-natural nut butter (such as peanut, almond, or cashew)

½ cup finely ground walnuts

1 cup Very Berry Chia Seed Jam (page 40) and/or vegan chocolate chips

Directions

1. Preheat the oven to 375°F. Line a rimmed baking sheet with parchment paper or a silicone mat.

2. In a large bowl, whisk together the oat flour, almond flour, tapioca starch, baking powder, and salt.

3. In a medium bowl, whisk together the coconut sugar, applesauce, and nut butter until smooth and creamy. Add the wet mixture to the dry mixture and mix until well combined.

4. Put the finely ground walnuts in a shallow dish. Roll the dough into golf ball–size balls. Roll each ball in the walnuts, making sure to coat the entire cookie. Place the coated cookies on the lined baking sheet. With your finger or the handle of a large wooden spoon, poke a deep indentation into each cookie. Bake for 8–10 minutes or until the walnut coating begins to brown slightly.

5. Remove the cookies from the oven and immediately fill each warm cookie with about 1 tablespoon of jam or chocolate chips. Place the cookies on a wire rack to cool.

Apple Cranberry Crisp GF

The sweetness of apples and the tartness of cranberries create the perfect flavor balance for this autumn desert. We like to think of our apple cranberry crisp as a lazy pie with a cookie crust topping.

Prep Time: 20 minutes | Cook Time: 40 minutes | Yield: 8–10 servings

Fruit Filling

6 medium McIntosh, Cortland, and/or Honeycrisp apples, peeled, cored, and chopped into ½-inch chunks

2 cups fresh cranberries

Grated zest and juice of 1 orange

½ cup coconut sugar

2 tablespoons cornstarch

2 teaspoons ground cinnamon

1 teaspoon pure vanilla extract

Topping

¾ cup rolled oats (not quick oats; gluten-free if necessary)

½ cup walnuts

½ cup pitted dates, soaked

½ teaspoon ground cinnamon

Directions

1. Preheat the oven to 375°F.

2. In a large bowl, combine all the filling ingredients and toss well. Transfer the mixture to a 9 × 13-inch baking pan.

3. Combine the oats and walnuts in a food processor and blend until you achieve a grainy and coarse texture. Add the dates and cinnamon and process to form a sticky, grainy mixture. Scatter the topping mixture evenly over the fruit.

4. Cover with aluminum foil and bake for 30 minutes. Remove the foil and bake for another 10 minutes or until the topping is crispy and the filling is bubbly. Serve warm.

Old-Fashioned Pumpkin Pie

Ditch the rolling pin and enjoy this easy pumpkin pie for Thanksgiving—or anytime you get the urge! The cookie-style crust pairs beautifully with the rich flavor of the pumpkin filling.

Prep Time: 20 minutes | Cook Time: 50–55 minutes | Yield: 8–10 servings

Ingredients

Crust

1½ cups rolled oats (not quick oats; gluten-free if necessary)

1 cup walnuts

1 cup pitted dates, soaked

1–2 tablespoons unsweetened applesauce or unsweetened plant-based milk, plus more as needed

½ teaspoon ground cinnamon

Filling

½ cup walnuts

1 cup pitted dates, soaked

¾ cup unsweetened plant-based milk

2 tablespoons molasses

1 (15-ounce) can pumpkin puree

3 tablespoons cornstarch

2 teaspoons pumpkin pie spice, store-bought or homemade (page 67)

1 teaspoon pure vanilla extract

1 teaspoon ground cinnamon

¼ teaspoon sea salt

Directions

1. Preheat the oven to 350°F.

2. To make the crust, combine the oats and walnuts in a food processor and blend until you achieve a grainy, coarse texture. Add the dates, applesauce or milk, and cinnamon to form a dough that holds together when you press it. If it feels a bit dry, add more applesauce or milk, 1 tablespoon at a time, to reach a stickier consistency. Press the mixture into the bottom and sides of a 9-inch pie plate.

3. To make the filling, combine the walnuts, dates, milk, and molasses in a high-powered blender and blend until smooth and creamy. Add the pumpkin puree, cornstarch, pumpkin pie spice, vanilla, cinnamon, and salt and continue to blend until smooth.

4. Transfer the pumpkin mixture to the piecrust and spread evenly. Bake for 50–55 minutes. Cover the edges with aluminum foil or a pie shield after about 15 minutes of baking if the crust begins to get too dark. After baking, the pie will be too soft to cut; allow the pie to cool at room temperature for 30 minutes, then transfer to the refrigerator to chill for 4–6 hours before serving.

Old-Fashioned
Pumpkin Pie

No-Bake Coconut
Pumpkin Pie (page 227)

Apple Cranberry
Crisp (page 253)

Acknowledgments

Creating mouth-watering recipes has been my passion since I was a young child. I would like to thank everyone who has guided me through this journey from the very beginning.

My husband, Nelson, has been my biggest fan. He has pushed my skills in the culinary world beyond what I ever imagined. His challenges seemed impossible at times, but thank you, Nelson, for giving me the confidence to do everything I do.

I would also like to thank my sister, Karen Whiston, who taught me how to cook as a young child and who has been by my side throughout every cookbook. Your optimism and encouragement, Karen, have kept me motivated every step of the way.

And a very special thanks to our children, Whitney, Colin, and Laura, for always giving me encouragement and love. You three are my world!

I also owe a debt of gratitude to our many PlantPure followers. So many people in this community have tested, tasted, and loved these recipes and given me the encouragement to write another cookbook. I have also been inspired by their passion for sharing the message around food, health, environment, animals, and sustainability. I have learned so much from all of you!

Of course, I also want to thank the BenBella team for guiding me through the publishing process. I consider you friends and have enjoyed working with all of you on every cookbook we've published.

Finally, I would like to thank Karen and Colin Campbell for teaching me everything there is to know about food and nutrition. Without these two pioneers I would never have this amazing opportunity to be a resource to everyone who wants to regain their health and live their best life.

Recipe Index

Subject Index

About the Author

Kim Campbell is the author of *The PlantPure Nation* and *The PlantPure Kitchen* cookbooks. She developed more than 250 delicious whole food, plant-based recipes using no processed oils. Kim is also the director of culinary education and development at PlantPure, where she develops new food products and delivers educational programming.

Kim graduated from Cornell University with a BS in human service studies and a concentration in nutrition and child development. She taught in elementary and middle school classrooms for over ten years. Her passion has always been nutrition education for children, families, and adults. Kim has been a plant-based cook for more than thirty-five years, cooking for her family and friends. Her love of culinary arts goes back to her early childhood growing up in a large traditional family. Kim is gifted at creating traditional American cuisine using 100 percent accessible plant-based ingredients. She builds flavors and textures that are familiar to most people, helping to make the transition to a plant-based diet easier for people.